The Complete Encyclopedia of
Wild Game & Fish Cleaning & Cooking

by Pat Billmeyer

Volume 1 — Big Game

Illustrated Butchering,
Skinning, Smoking, Canning,
Tanning, Cooking & Drying

★ yesnaby publishers

r.d. 8, box 213
danville, pa 17821

Copyright © 1983 by Pat Billmeyer

Published by Yesnaby Publishers, R.D. 8, Box 213, Danville, Pa. 17821

All rights reserved. No part of this book may be reproduced in any manner without written permission from the publisher, except by reviewers who may quote brief passages to be printed in a magazine or newspaper.

Printed and bound in the United States of America.

Library of Congress Catalog Number: 83-50091

International Standard Book Number: 0-9606262-3-9
(Set)
0-9606262-4-7
(Volume)

To my son and editor, **Mark William Hintz**. Without his talent, energy, skill, persistence, patience and will, this book would never have been published.

Contents

CHAPTER 1   BIG GAME FIELD DRESSING   1-11
   Gutting...Skinning...Skinning When Head is not to be Trophy Mounted...Skinning When Head is to be Trophy Mounted... Aging

CHAPTER 2   BUTCHERING BIG GAME   12-20
   Butchering the Forequarters...Butchering the Hindquarters

CHAPTER 3   BIG GAME CANNING, DRYING & SMOKING   21-36
   Preparation of Meat...Raw Pack...Hot Pack... Jerky...Drying...Smoking... Salting...Smokehouses...Tanning... Buckskin...Rawhide...Hard Hide Curing

CHAPTER 4   BIG GAME DELICACIES   37-47
   Kidneys...Tongue...Liver...Heart...Brains ...Corned...Mincemeat...Spareribs...Sausage

CHAPTER 5   BIG GAME RECIPES   48-69
   All about Venison...Antelope...Elk... Deer...Buffalo...Goat...Moose...Sheep ...Bear...Javelina or Wild Pig...Game Sauces

CHAPTER 6   BIG GAME RECIPES JUST FOR FUN   70-76

A BRIEF HISTORY OF USING FIRE TO 77-78
    PREPARE MEAT

IN DEFENSE OF HUNTING (OR, ANN 79-81
    LANDERS EAT YOUR HEART OUT!)

Foreword

The right to hunt game is a precious American Freedom which was forbidden to any except the king and his buddies in old England. From an old English cookbook published in 1861 comes the following excerpt.

"The Common Law of England says that goods, in which no person can claim any property, belong, by his or her perogative, to the king or queen. Accordingly, those animals which come under the denomination of Game are styled his or her majesty's, and may be granted by the sovereign to another. There are innumerable acts of parliament inflicting penalties on persons who may illegally kill game, and some of them are very severe." (Death)

Since we each have the rights of a sovereign in America, let us hunt with skill, perseverance and self-discipline, and prepare and cook well each life we have taken to sustain our own.

Every moving thing that liveth shall be meat for you: even as the green herb have I given you all things.

Genesis, 9:3

Big Game Field Dressing

Chapter 1

Gutting

THESE DIRECTIONS MAY BE FOLLOWED FOR ALL BIG GAME LISTED EXCEPT THE WILD PIG OR WILD BOAR, COLLARD PECCARY, JAVELINA OR MUSK HOG. See those directions under the specific animal.

More meat has been ruined by mishandling in the field than any other single cause. The hunter should read and remember the following directions:

Gut your kill immediately, using a sharp knife. Roll the animal over on its back with the rump lower than the shoulders and spread the hind legs. Make a cut along the center of the belly from the breastbone to within several inches of the milk bag or testicles.

First, cut through the hide, then through the belly muscle. Don't cut into the intestines. AVOID CUTTING OR BREAKING THE BLADDER. Cut around the milk bag or testicles. See Illustration #1 on following page.

Big Game

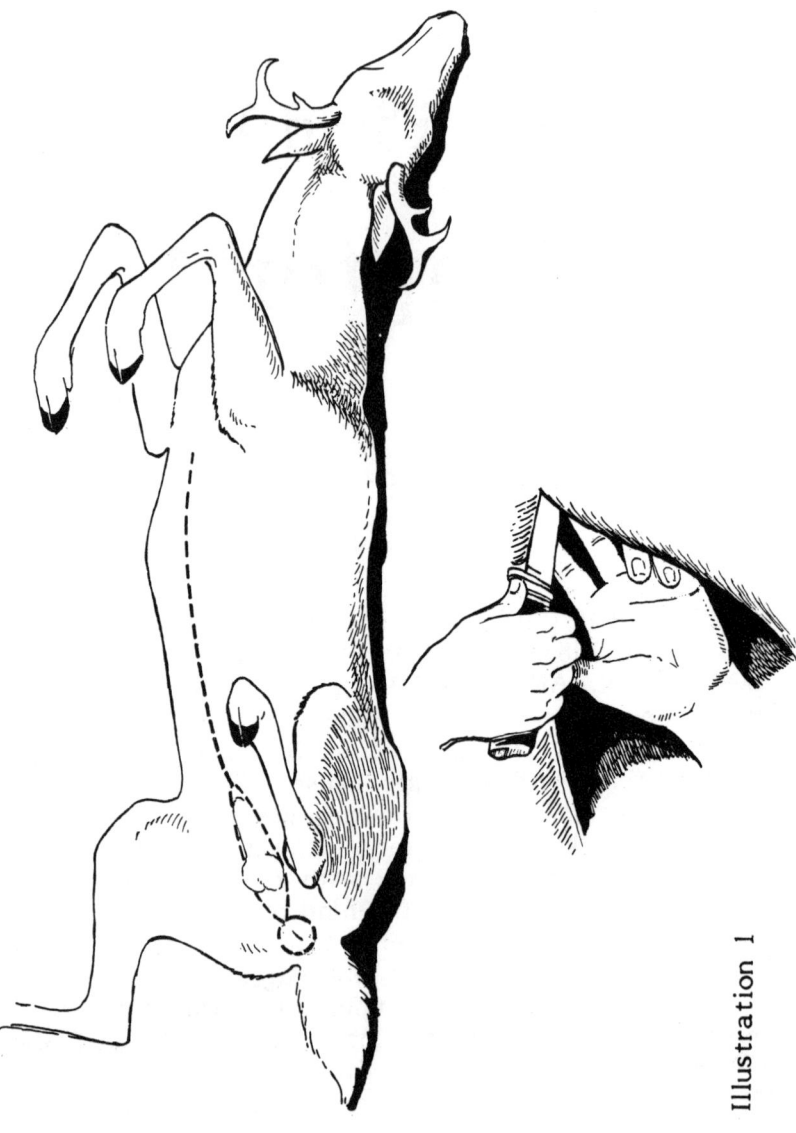

Illustration 1

Chapter One

Insert knife 3-4 inches deep between the anus and pelvic bone and cut around the anus, taking care not to cut into it.

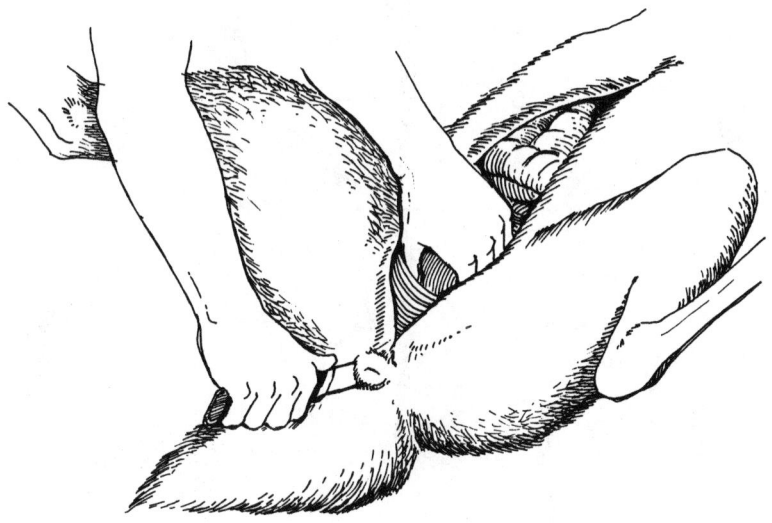

Illustration 2

Big Game

Reach inside and pull through the anus and bladder. Loosen and roll out the stomach and intestines.

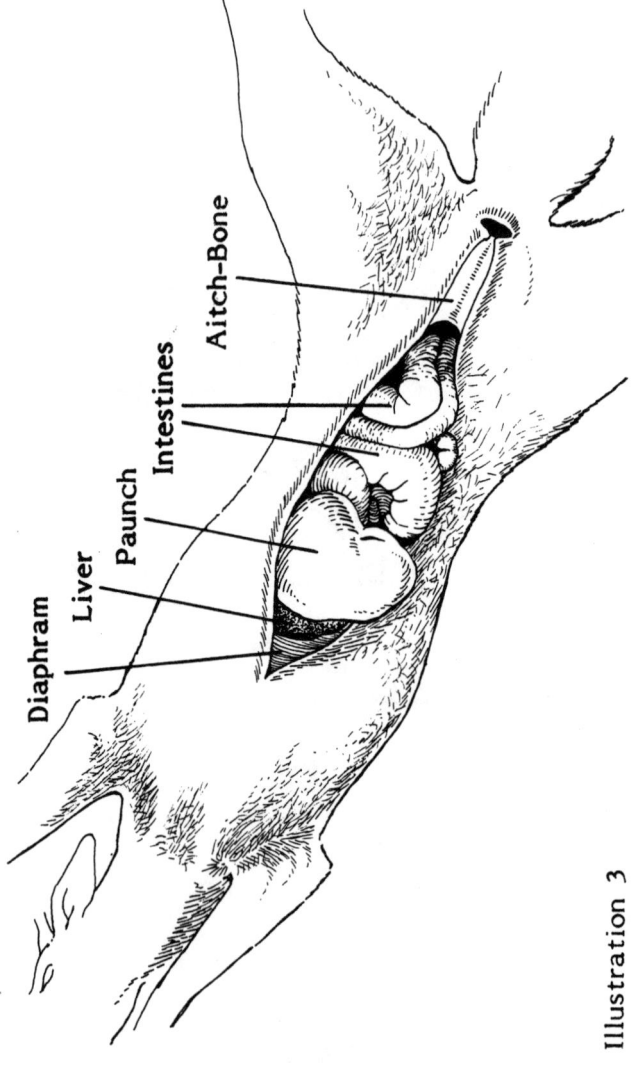

Illustration 3

Chapter One

Cut around the edge of the diaphragm which separates the chest and stomach cavities, then reach forward to cut the windpipe and gullet ahead of the lungs. Now, pull the lungs and heart from the chest cavity. Save the heart and liver, they're good! Drain all excess blood by turning the body face down.

If you have punctured the guts, wipe the cavity as clean as possible or flush it out with water and dry. DON'T WASH WITH WATER UNLESS THE GUTS ARE BADLY SHOT UP. THE IMPORTANT POINT IS TO REMOVE THE GUTS IMMEDIATELY AFTER THE KILL WITHOUT CONTAMINATING THE BODY CAVITY WITH DIRT, HAIR OR CONTENTS OF THE DIGESTIVE TRACT. ALSO, DRAIN EXCESS BLOOD FROM THE CAVITY.

On a deer, immediately remove the tufts and gland on the forepart of the back legs. They are spongy, contain urine, and must be cut out immediately.

HANG THE CARCASS AND COOL IT AS QUICKLY AS POSSIBLE. Hang it **in the shade** and prop the flanks open with sticks to permit air circulation in the body cavity. The air case hardens the surface and protects the exposed meat.

NEVER TIE THE DEER TO THE CAR WHERE ENGINE HEAT CAN CAUSE THE MEAT TO DETERIORATE. You may use a car top carrier or put it in the trunk.

The game commission says it is best to leave the hide on to protect the meat. My butcher, who has processed thousands of deer, antelope, etc. says he advises that the animal be skinned the same day it is shot so the body heat escapes. Your situation will have to dictate your course to follow here.

We often take our big game to a locker plant or a butcher for cutting up. We always direct our butcher to mix our ground meat with beef suet (fat) or pork

Big Game

fat. It gives a delicious taste and guards against dryness. If your family is not used to game, have the butcher cut out only the most tender chops, steaks and roasts and grind all the rest and mix it with suet. It can be used in chili con carne, meat loaf, spaghetti sauce, meat balls, etc.

Make sure the butcher hangs the big game for two to four weeks. If it has hung for a considerable time at the hunting camp, the time it has hung and the temperature during that time must be discussed with the butcher.

There are times when getting the venison to a butcher is impractical, and surely any serious hunter should know how to butcher his or her hard won prize.

Skinning

First, you must cut off the legs at the first joint. Start with the hind legs, cut the skin around the joint and break the joint, then cut off. Take care not to cut the tendon above the joint because that is ideal to hang the animal for skinning. Using the same procedure, cut off the forelegs and hang the animal as illustrated.

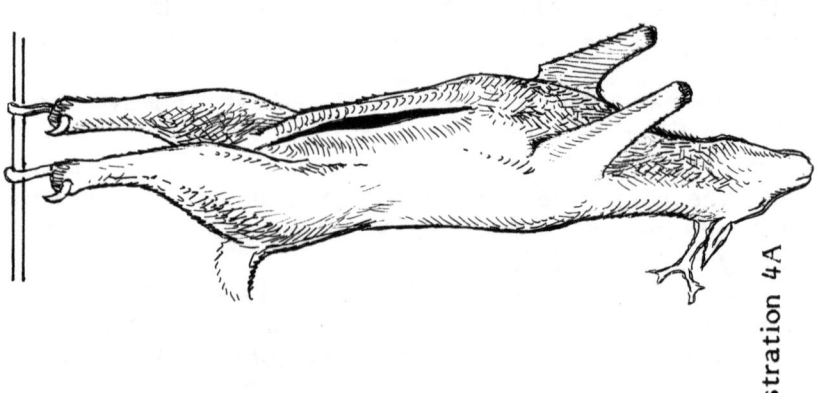

Illustration 4A

Chapter One

WHEN THE HEAD IS NOT TO BE TROPHY MOUNTED

Extend the belly cut up the chest and up the neck to the head   (see Illustration).Cut the skin from the belly cut to the end of the front legs on the inside of the legs. Cut the skin from the anus area to the ends of the back legs on the INSIDE of the legs.

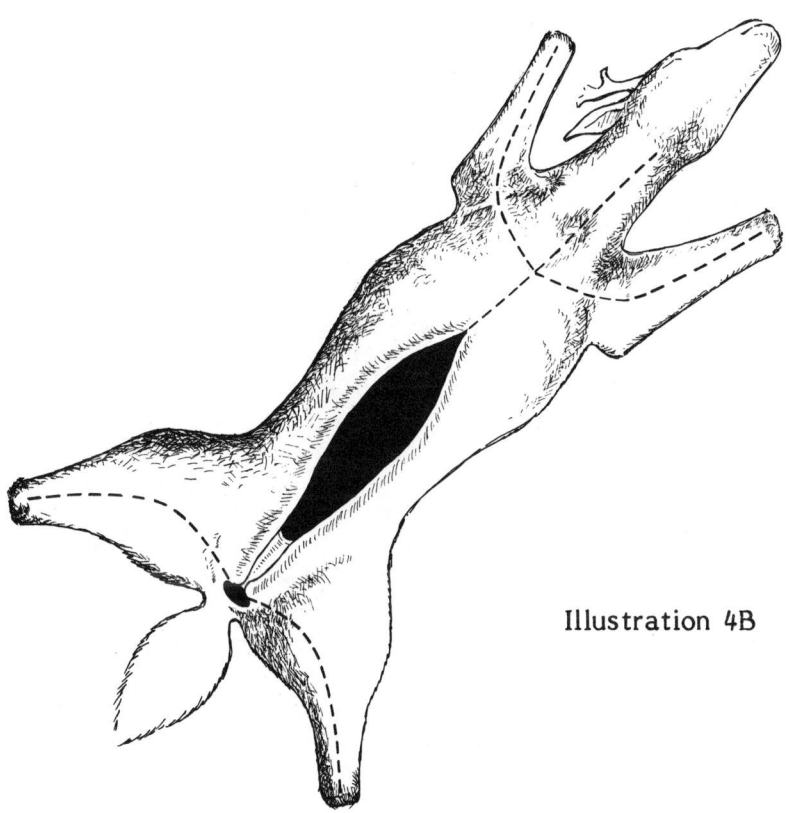

Illustration 4B

Big Game

Work the skin loose from the belly and flank, taking care not to pierce the skin or meat. Repeat with the hind legs, then the front legs. Always hold the end of the skin tightly, pulling it away from the carcass. If the skin is to be used for a rug or a wallcovering, skin out the tail; otherwise cut off the tail at the base of the spine. Pull the skin entirely off around the neck to the head. Cut around the neck between the first vertebra and the skull and twist and cut until the head comes off.

Before proceeding with the butchering there are a few general rules I want you to hold in mind.

WHEN THE HEAD IS TO BE TROPHY MOUNTED

The first step is the same as conventional skinning, that is, you cut off the legs at the first joint. Start with the hind legs, cut the skin around the joint and break the joint, then cut off. Take care not to cut the tendon above the joint because that is ideal to hang the animal for skinning. Using the same procedure, cut off the forelegs and hang the animal as in illustration 4A.

Now, consult Illustration 5 on the following page.

Start your cut several inches behind the shoulder and cut all around the carcass, then cut the skin following the spine to the head. Cut the skin on the inside of the legs up to the center cut.

Using the knife handle, an antler or a similar blunt instrument, skin the animal, starting with the forelegs, until you have it skinned to its Adam's apple and atlas joint (between the head and the first joint of the spine.) Cut through the neck and twist, then complete

Chapter One

cutting off the head. Get it to the taxidermist immediately.

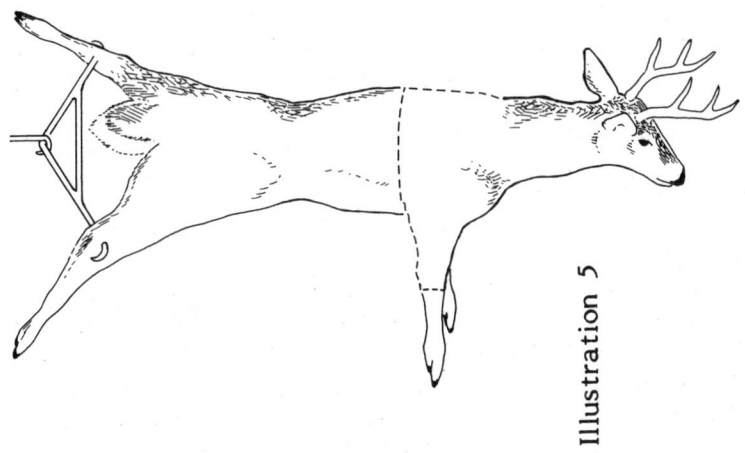

Illustration 5

IF YOU CAN'T GET IT TO THE TAXIDERMIST AT ONCE, YOU MUST PEEL THE SKULL IN THE FOLLOWING FASHION:

CAREFULLY cut around the skin at the base of the antlers. Cut the skin loose from the forehead to the eye sockets and loosen the skin around the eye sockets. Continue skinning down toward the nose, along the jaws, nostrils and lips, until completely free of the skull. Great care must be exercised that you do not pierce the skin because much of this part cannot be repaired by the taxidermist.

Next, saw through the skull across the eye sockets. Saw down through the skull about an inch behind the antlers.

Big Game

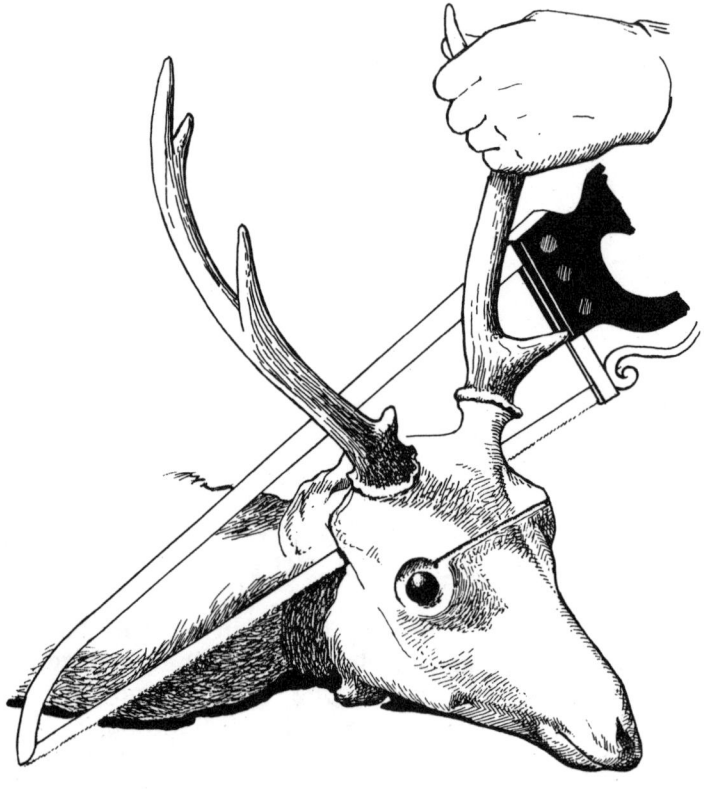

Illustration 6

Chapter One

Trim off all the meat from the antler base or put it in a pot of water and boil it off. Take the entire skin and antlers to the taxidermist.

To sum up, don't skimp by cutting too high on the neck, the taxidermist needs this extra skin. Get it to the taxidermist immediately. Be super careful when skinning the face because if you break through this skin you create big problems for the taxidermist.

Continue skinning out the lower half of the skin following the directions given for conventional skinning. Remove the brains and cook them, following my instructions under brains. (Consult index).

AGING

The venison should be aged (hung) at temperatures of 36-40 degrees. One week is usual for a very young animal and two to three weeks for older animals. Include in this time period any time it hung at the hunting camp.

Many experts say you should get the hide off as soon as possible. Others insist the hide should be left on during aging. I have noticed that venison aged with the hide on definitely has a stronger taste than that aged with the hide off.

I think a sensible rule is to leave the hide on while at the hunting camp and while transporting it (never on the hood of a car where the engine heat ruins it before you go ten miles).

As soon as the animal can be skinned and hung in a protected, cool place where it will not be subjected to insects or marauding animals, it should be done. Leaving the hide on longer than necessary does not improve the taste.

Butchering Big Game

Chapter 2

Using a sharp meat saw, cut off the forequarters directly behind the shoulder, between the 4th and 5th ribs, as illustrated in Illustration 7A.

Cut and saw off the ribcage and the back bone from the hind legs as shown in Illustration 7B.

Chapter Two

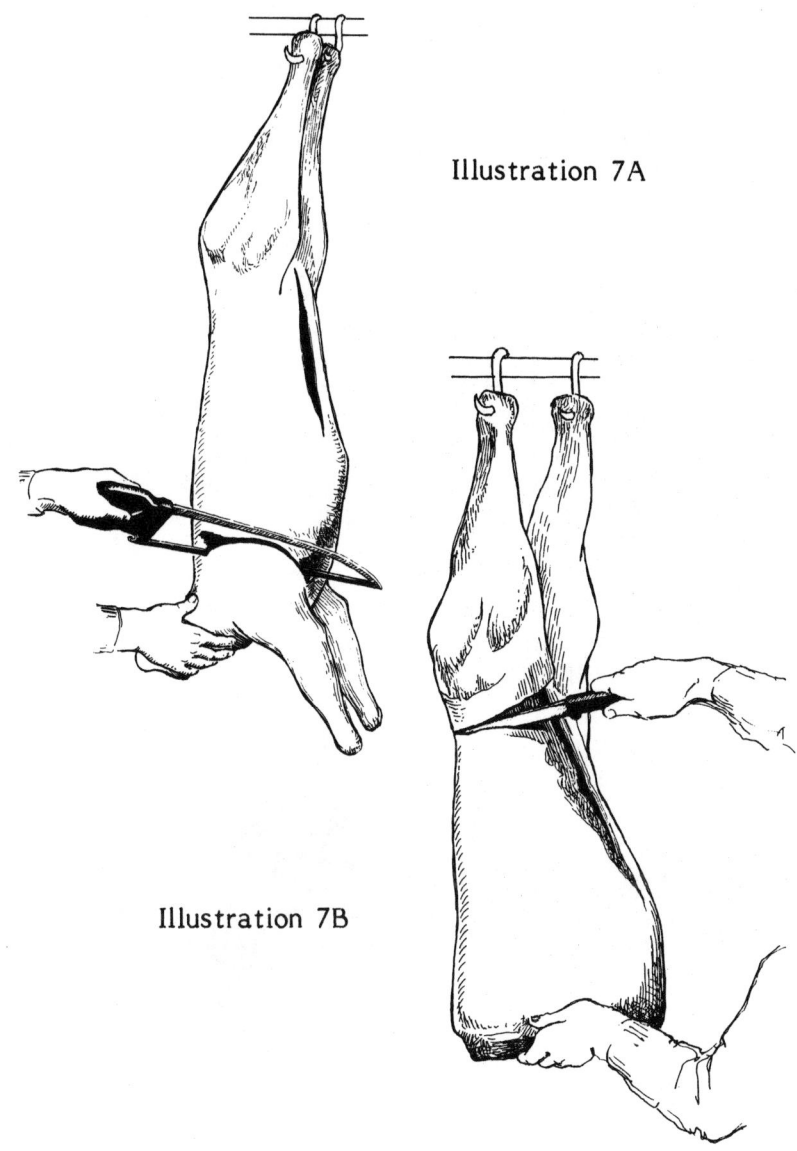

Illustration 7A

Illustration 7B

Big Game

Illustration 7c is what we're heading for.

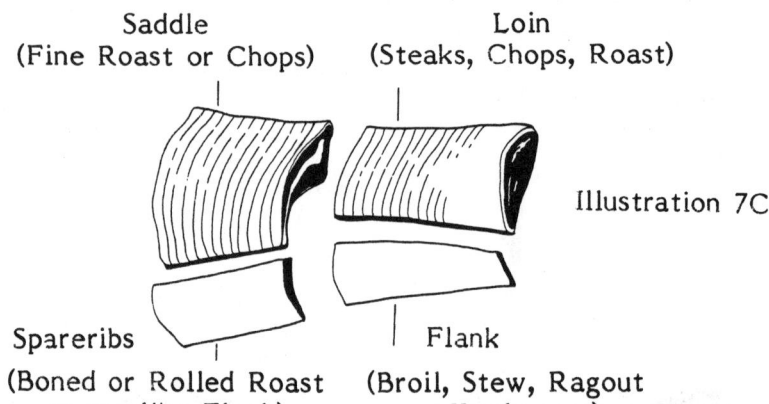

Saddle
(Fine Roast or Chops)

Loin
(Steaks, Chops, Roast)

Illustration 7C

Spareribs
(Boned or Rolled Roast
or use like Flank)

Flank
(Broil, Stew, Ragout
or Hamburger)

Place the center section on a secure stand and cut and saw through the ribs- 6 to 9 inches from the backbone (depending on the size of the animal) and parallel to it as in Illustration 8.

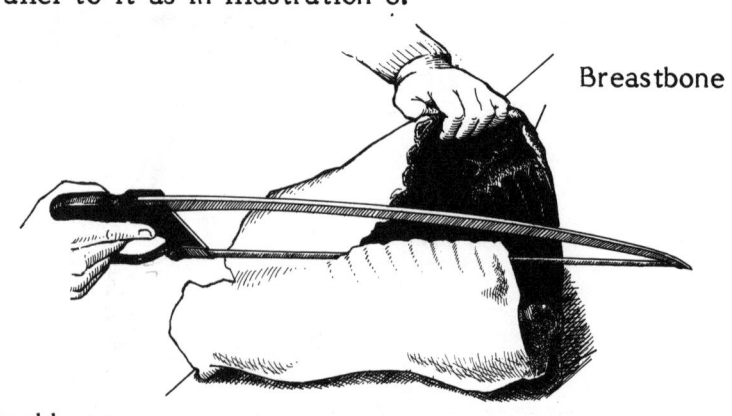

Breastbone

Backbone

Illustration 8

Chapter Two

The spareribs are now removed from the back.
Remove the kidneys and place them in salt water to draw out the urine taste. (Soak overnight before freezing for use later or prepare as indicated under KIDNEYS. See Index.)
Saw down the middle of the back with a handsaw as shown in Illustration 9.

Backbone

Illustration 9

This is easier done if the back is slightly frozen. Cut and saw the chops and steaks from both halves. Sprinkle with meat tenderizer if desired. Wrap them in individual or family sized portions and freeze.

Big Game

Split the breast bone with either a knife or saw (depending on the age of the animal), as in Illustration 10.

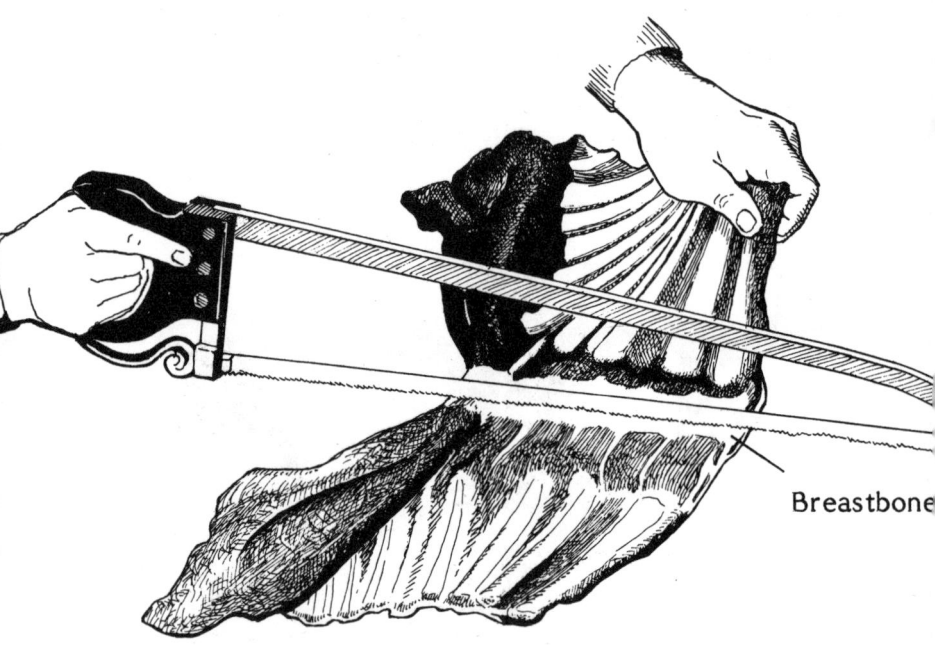

Breastbone

Illustration 10

Trim off the lower 2 inches of breastbone so the spareribs may be cut either separately or in family sized pieces. Sprinkle with meat tenderizer if desired. Wrap and freeze or cook by my directions under spareribs. See index.

Chapter Two

Butchering the Forequarters

Place the forequarters on a secure stand on its back. The following illustration is what we are heading for.

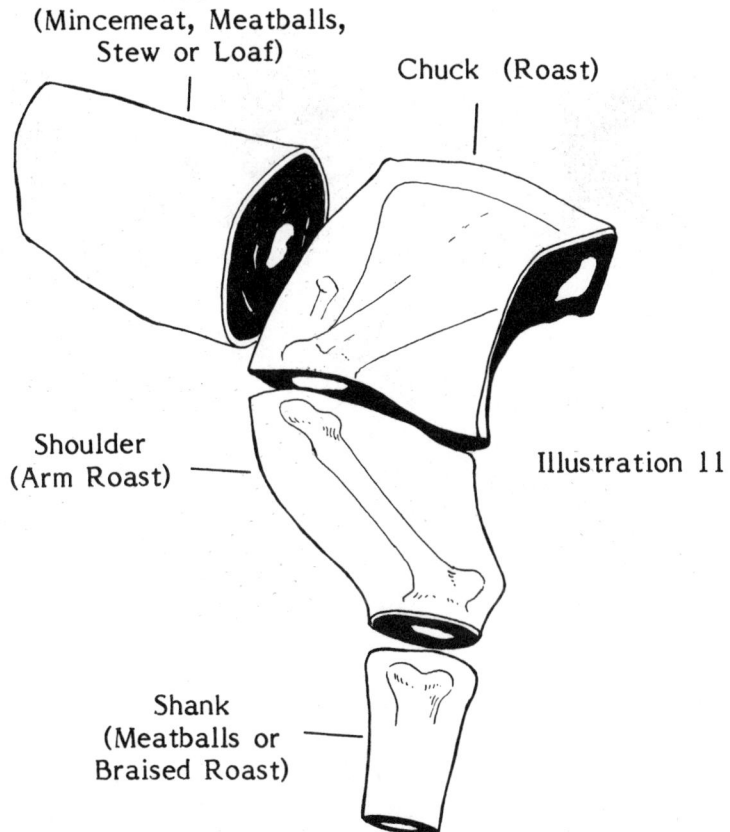

Illustration 11

Cut straight up the center and remove the windpipe as in Illustration 12.

Big Game

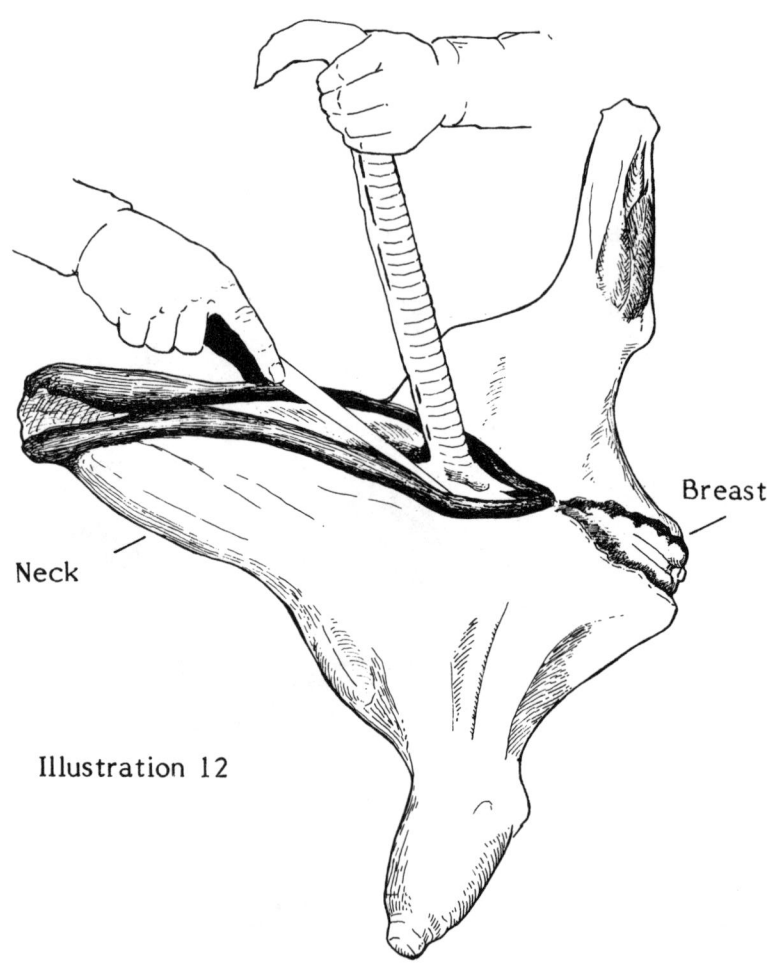

Illustration 12

Bone out the chest and neck, then the shoulder blade. The most important thing to know about this procedure is that under the shoulder blade is the PRE-SCAPULAR GLAND that MUST BE REMOVED or it will destroy the flavor of the meat. You must find and remove it without piercing it. It may be covered with fat. See Illustration 13.

Chapter Two

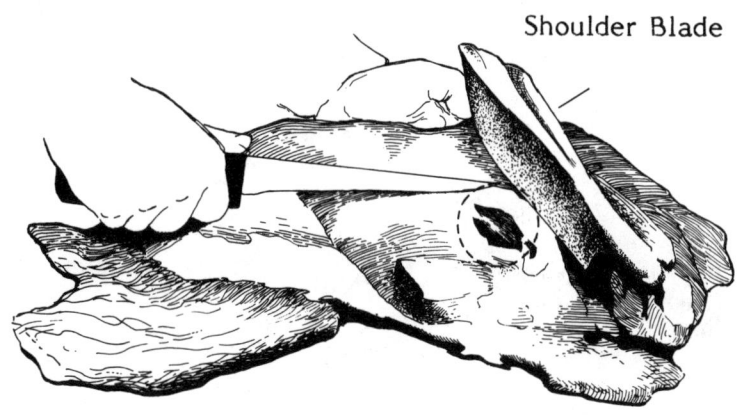

Illustration 13

Bone, and remove the backstrap tendon at the center of the neck.

Cut off the lower parts of the leg (shank) and use it in one piece for braised pot roast (see index), or bone it and grind or chop the meat for hamburger. Wrap and freeze.

Cut off the shoulder arm roast at the joint as shown in Illustration 11. Wrap and freeze.

If you want a boneless chuck roast, bone out the chest and neck, trim off the fat (if any) and sprinkle with meat tenderizer if desired. Tuck the neck meat down and roll up tightly, tie with twine, wrap and freeze. You can also grind the boned neck meat for hamburger.

Big Game

Butchering the Hindquarters

Put the hindquarters on its back on a secure stand. Illustration 14 is our goal.

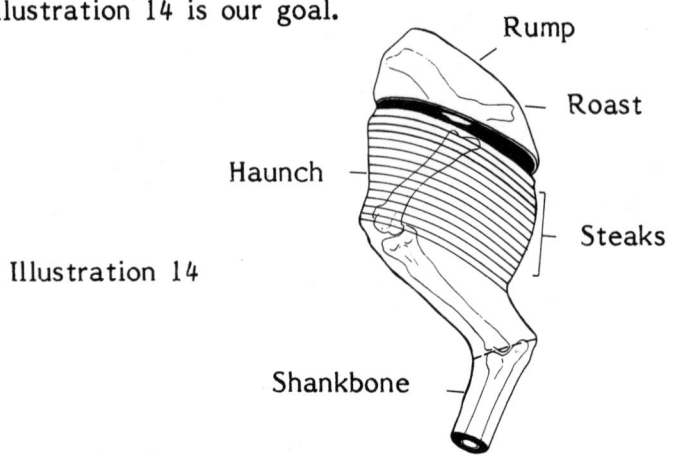

Illustration 14

Remove the lower legs by cutting around the pelvic bone and cut the thighbone from its socket. Trim and discard the pelvic bone.

Cut off the shank part of the legs at the joints. If you have not removed the popliteal (flank) glands while field dressing, do it now, without piercing the gland. Carefully wash your hands, the knife and that part of the meat before proceeding.

Trim off the fat and loose meat from the ham. Using a sharp knife and a saw, cut the steaks as shown in Illustration 14. It helps if the ham is barely frozen for this procedure.

Take the remaining ham, cut lengthwise along the thighbone and remove. Sprinkle the meat with tenderizer if desired. Roll up the meat and tie it with twine for a rolled roast. You may bone the rump roasts or leave the bone in. Sprinkle with tenderizer and freeze.

Big Game Canning, Drying & Smoking

Chapter 3

Canning

I must say I am partial to canned game. If it is done properly it tastes like a delicious pot roast and your preparation is all done when it comes time to get the meal. Just open the can and heat, make gravy with the juices, whip up the mashed potatoes or Yorkshire pudding and you're an instant hero or heroine. Canning the meat also naturally tenderizes it.

PREPARATION OF MEAT

The one critical point to remember when canning game is to remove the fat. The fat has a strong taste which will intensify with canning, so be careful here. Also, remove all bones and cut into can-size (or smaller) pieces, depending on what you're working with.

Big Game

RAW PACK

You must take one extra step when raw canning meat: EXHAUST or preheat the meat IN THE CAN OR JAR to 170 degree F. temperature. This drives out any air in the meat or jar and gives you a firm seal. It's actually a simple process.

In Jars

Push the meat rather firmly into jars, leaving 1 inch of headroom. Add no water - it will make its own liquid.

In Cans

Push the meat rather firmly into the jars, leaving NO headroom.

Exhausting (the jars, not you)

Place filled, OPEN jars or cans on a rack in a kettle and add water up to about 2 inches below the tops of the container. Cover the kettle and slow boil for 70 to 75 minutes - until the temperature in the center of the meat reaches 170 degrees F. Add 1/2 teaspoon of salt to each pint or #2 or #2 1/2 can, 1 teaspoon of salt to each quart.

HOT PACK (Precooked)

Prepare as indicated above. If you want to brown it (I always do) simply brown it under a broiler or in a frying pan. Do not dredge it in flour first.

Put the meat in a large pan and add 1 to 1 1/2 inches of water. COVER and simmer in a 350° oven or on the top of the stove for about 1/2 hour after it has

Chapter Three

come to a boil.

In Jars

Immediately pack hot meat into jars. Add 1/2 teaspoon of salt per pint, 1 teaspoon of salt per quart. Add boiling meat juices or water if necessary, leaving 1 inch of headroom. Wipe the jar top clean and put on the lid. Pressure process at 10 pounds $240°$ F. for 75 minutes for pints and 90 minutes for quarts. Remove and complete the seal if necessary.

In Cans

Immediately pack hot meat into cans. Add 1/2 teaspoon of salt to each #2 or #2 1/2 can and fill cans TO THE TOP with the boiling juices or water if needed. Wipe can rims and seal. Pressure process at 10 pounds ($240°$ F.) for #2 cans for 65 minutes and 10 pounds ($240°$ F.) #2 1/2 cans for 90 minutes.

Drying

Use the leanest muscle meat for this. Make sure no fat or gristle remains on the meat. Cut long strips lengthwise of the grain, an inch wide and 1/2 inch thick.

UNPICKLED JERKY

Lay strips out on a board. Using a rolling pin or a meat mallet, pound in salt, pepper and any other herbs or spices you like. Do not use more than 1 teaspoon of salt per pound of meat. Proceed with a drying method of your choice listed below.

Big Game

PICKLED JERKY

Mix 3 quarts of water with 2 cups of pickling salt. (We get this salt at our country grocery store. Farmers' supply stores, such as Agway, also have it.) Soak the cut strips in a cool place for at least 24 hours. Remove and wipe dry. Proceed with a drying method of your choice listed below.

If I were going to carry the jerky on hiking trips, I would probably pickle it before I dried it, because salt does cure meat more thoroughly, but the Indians and early frontiersmen did not salt their jerky.

However you have presalted it, the drying is the same.

OVEN DRYING

Lay out prepared strips on oven racks, making sure they are not touching each other. Put them into a 100 to 120 degree F. oven. Leave the door propped open an inch or two and process for 5 hours. Turn them over and continue processing for about 5 more hours. It will look terrible when it is done - very dark and shriveled - and you can test it by taking out a piece and cooling it, then trying to snap it. It should be brittle, like a green stick, not overdried until it snaps off. Wrap it in foil or a clear wrapper and store in a cool place in a covered container.

DRYING OVER COALS

The prepared strips must be suspended about 4 feet above a VERY LOW bed of coals. You do not want the meat to cook or smoke, so hardwood or charcoal is preferable. This method could take up to 24 hours depending on the variables such as thickness of strips, heat of fire, etc. Use the test for doneness listed above under Oven Drying.

DRYING IN THE SUN

Prepare as listed above under unpickled or pickled jerky. The old fashioned jerky was never salted but salting does add an element of safety. Choose your weather wisely. You must have several days of clear weather with good sun and a gentle breeze. The Indians built stick platforms 5 or 6 feet high and simply suspended the strips of meat from it until it was dry. If it rained before it was dry they threw bark or a skin over it. I must say, this is my least favorite form of preserving meat because it is nearly impossible to control sanitation and you have great danger of losing your meat entirely if inclement weather intervenes. If you do it anyway, use the test for doneness listed under Oven Drying, and cover it with cheesecloth during the process to keep the flies and other insects off.

Smoking

Smoking game is done to improve the taste by adding the delicious smoky flavor, dry the surface of the meat and discourage insects. The real "curing" or limiting the bacterial growth in the meat is accomplished by inserting salt deep into the tissues; therefore, any instructions on smoking must begin with the "salt bath".

THE BRINE

For every 25 pounds of venison mix:

1 gallon water

Big Game

3 cups coarse pickling salt
1 cup sugar
1 tablespoon of saltpeter (this only protects the color of the meat, it does nothing to inhibit bacteria growth.)

    Dissolve this thoroughly in a well-sterilized crock or barrel. Place the BONED meat into the solution and place a weighted plate or board over the meat to keep it submerged. Even a small piece of meat sticking out of the solution can cause the entire crock of meat to spoil so make sure it is all well covered. Cover the vessel carefully and place it where it will have a storage temperature of 38 degrees F. The salt penetrates too slowly if the temperature goes below 36 degrees F. and if it goes much higher than 38 degrees F. it greatly increases the chance of spoiling. Do not try to salt and smoke prefrozen meat.
    It must be left in the brine for four weeks. At the end of each 7 days remove the meat and thoroughly stir the brine, then repack the meat, carefully weight down and cover. If at any time you discover the brine smells sour or has become sirupy or "ropy", remove the meat and scrub it well with clean water; discard the brine and scrub and scald the meat crock. Make FRESH brine and repeat the above.

DRY SALTING

This is worth the trouble in warmer climates.
For each 25 pounds of venison mix:

3 cups coarse pickling salt
1 cup white or brown sugar
1 tablespoon saltpeter (this protects the color of the meat, it does nothing to cure it.)

Rub this well into the surface of the BONED venison. (The greatest number of failures involve meat with the bone left in where the salt does not penetrate. You can save yourself a lot of trouble by removing the bone before pickling and smoking.) Sprinkle a layer of the mixture in the bottom of a sterilized crock or barrel. Add the pieces of salt-coated meat. Make sure there is salt between each piece and then sprinkle the rest of the salt mixture on top. Cover it with a loose fitting cover and/or cheesecloth and allow it to cure for 4 weeks. At the end of each week remove the cover and sprinkle 1/2 of the above mixture under, around and over each piece of meat. The crock must be kept in a cool place - 36 to 38 degrees F. As a rule of thumb, cure it 2 days for each pound of venison.

The Smokehouse

In my section of the country every house used to have a smokehouse which was built like Illustration 15.

My husband said crawling in and out of this smokehouse three times a day made him smell like a smoked ham for the entire time he was smoking meat. Therefore, he says this next plan is a great idea. You have to get hold of a 50 gallon barrel with one end cut out. If it has contained oil, set it on fire, then scour it thoroughly. See Illustration 16.

Fit a stove pipe elbow into a hole cut into the bottom of the barrel and extend a pipe down to the fire pit about ten feet away. Put a metal cover over the fire pit; and if children or small animals are around it is wise to build a temporary restraining fence around it, you don't want anyone falling into it! Lay some two

Big Game

by fours or sturdy sticks over the top of the drum and a rather loose fitting cover over that. You want it loose enough to carry off the moisture and make a draft so the fire won't go out in the fire pit.

A very simple smoker can be made out of big wooden packing boxes as shown in Illustration 17. May I say I don't approve of this kind because the danger of fire is very great, even if you keep the fire tiny and smoky, the way you are supposed to. For the sake of the old homestead, if you do build this one, put it a long way from any other structure. Build the fire in a metal container.

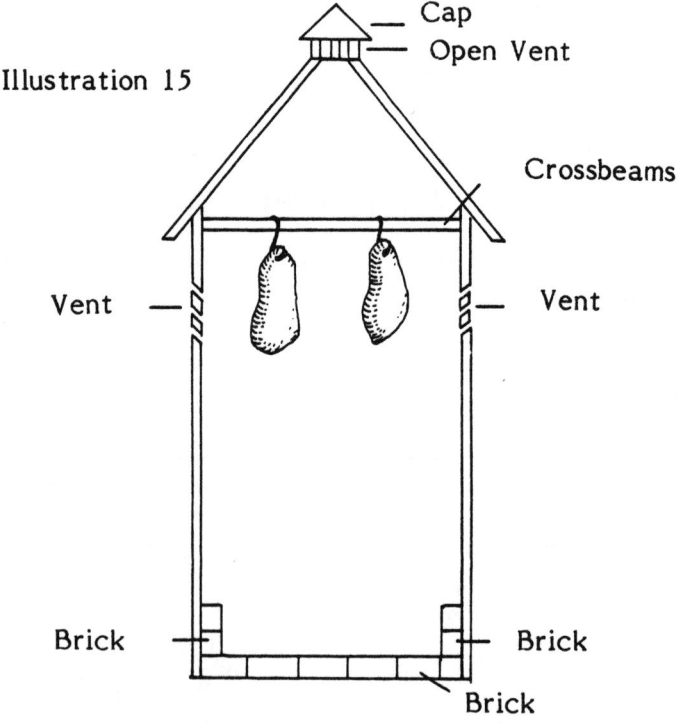

OLD-FASHIONED SMOKEHOUSE

Chapter Three

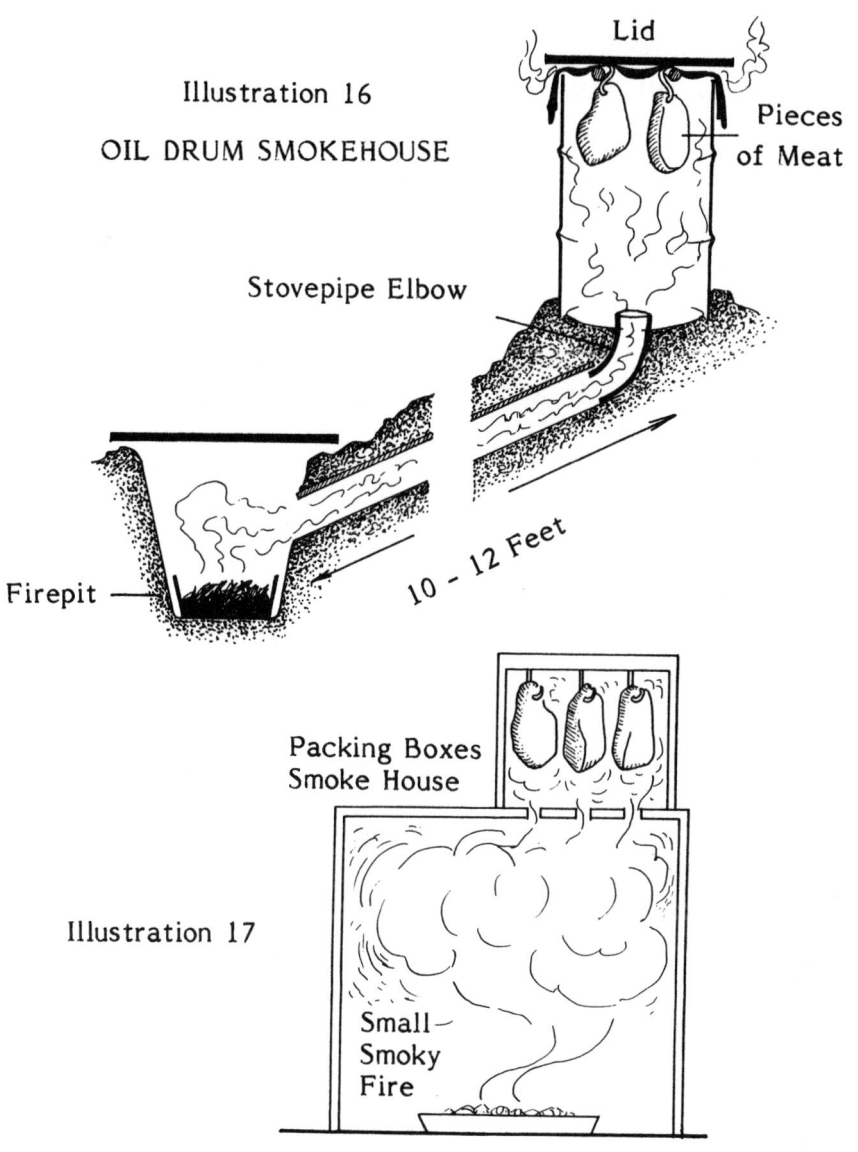

Illustration 16
OIL DRUM SMOKEHOUSE

Illustration 17

"CHEAPIE" SMOKEHOUSE

Big Game

BUILDING THE FIRE

You must use only hardwoods or "field corn" corncobs. The pine or softwoods ruin the taste of the meat. Do not use a chemical starter, or the meat will taste of it. Crisscross small pieces of very dry hardwood and bark to get started. Get your fire well established before you put in the meat so you don't ruin the meat with too hot a fire right at the beginning. Hang a thermometer where your meat will be and make sure it's a smoky ideal 90 degrees F. If it goes up as high as 100 to 120 degrees F. it will survive, but 90 degrees F. is best. This is much easier to maintain if the temperature outside stays from 30 to 50 degrees F.

PREPARE THE VENISON

Remove it from the crock and scrub off the surface salt, then hang it in a cool, dry place until the outside is dry - not longer than 24 hours. Run a strong wire through one end of the meat, deep enough so it will support its weight. Hang it to the supports.

TIMING

The time you must leave it in the smokehouse depends on the size of the pieces of venison and how well you keep an even, dense smoke. It will run from 50 to 70 hours.

FINAL WORD ON SMOKING

I do not like injecting "liquid smoke" or "smoke salt"; therefore, I am not giving any directions on using them. I dislike adding chemicals and I do not like their taste. Also, I feel they may give a false sense of

Chapter Three

security and they are in no way beneficial for "curing" venison.

There is another way to smoke venison called "hot smoking" which does not cure venison but which does give it a wonderful taste and cooks it. We purchased a smoker for this, but you could make your own. It is roughly constructed like the following illustration.

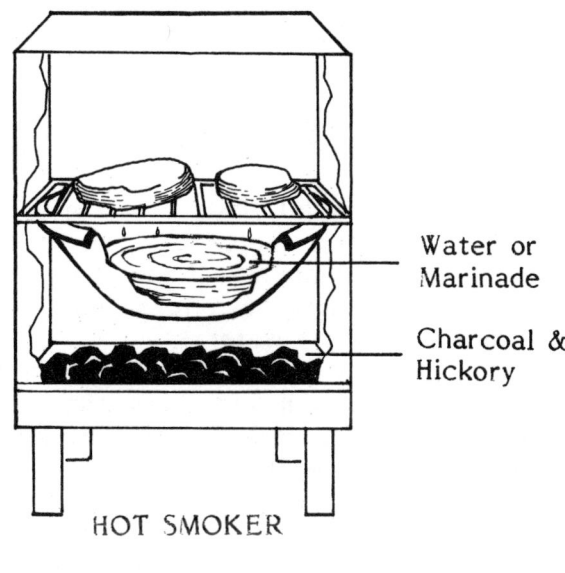

Illustration 18

The pieces of venison are smoked and cooked 6 to 8 hours until they are 160 degrees to 170 degrees F. This type of cooking tenderizes, cooks and smokes to perfection. It does not preserve, and if you want to keep it after it has been smoked this way, you must freeze it. I must say, venison smoked this way truly tastes "out of this world". It is divine.

The Hide — Tanning, Making Buckskin, Making Rawhide, & Hard Hide Curing

Mr. Dick Sutton of Benton, Pennsylvania, first place winner of the 1983 Fish and Reptile Skin Mount Competition of the Pennsylvania Taxidermist Association, kindly consented to advise me in this tanning and curing section.

TANNING THE HIDE (When you want the hair left on for rugs, etc.)

First, scrape all flesh from the inside of the skin, taking care not to pierce it. This is done most easily directly after skinning. If you have waited a day or two you'll probably have to soften the fleshy side of the hide with warm water.

After it is scraped clean, apply uniodized table salt to the flesh side, making sure that all the parts are covered. Fold it, flesh side to flesh side, roll it up and prop it up in an elevated position for 24 hours so the blood and body fluid drain out. Scrape it again.

TANNING FLUID

Mix in a washtub or large container:

5 gallons water
5 pounds uniodized table salt

Bring this to a boil, stirring. Carry this mixture outside and carefully add 5 ounces of sulphuric acid. We all know how dangerous sulphuric acid is, so use super care in handling it and DO NOT BREATHE IN the mixture. Immerse the entire hide in the fluid, being careful not to burn your hands, and leave it, COVERED, where children and pets won't get at it, for at least two weeks. Poke around in it with a big stick once or twice a day to make sure all parts are equally treated.

Remove the hide from the tanning liquor and rinse it carefully in an alkali bath (washing soda) then soak and rinse it in a fresh batch of washing soda for two hours. Remove it and dry off the fleshy side and rub it with oil - mineral oil, neatsfoot oil, vaseline, etc. The old timers used lard or bacon fat but this can draw varmints.

Hang it for several days so the oil penetrates the skin. Rub it again with oil once or twice if it needs it.

The last step is to soften the hide. To do this you must twist, pull and haul the moist hide over the edge of a sturdy pole until it is velvety soft. A clothesline pole should work, but wash the pole after use or your spouse may leave. This is not an easy job but do a thorough job or you've wasted all the rest of your work.

Next, smoke the hide to close the pores. You do not want flames or heat, just a small, smoky smudge pot.

You now have a soft, supple, well-tanned hide.

TO MAKE BUCKSKIN

First, scrape all the flesh from the inside of the skin, taking care not to pierce it. Then soak the hide for several days in the following dehairing solution.

5 gallons of water
1 quart wood ashes
1 quart slacked hydrated lime

Big Game

The Indians just wet the hide, rubbed wood ashes into the hair and rolled it up for a few days, but I won't vouch for that method.

Remove the hide from the solution and scrape off all the hair and black skin. Turn it over and scrape the other side clean.

Grease the fleshy side lightly with mineral oil, neat's-foot oil, vaseline, etc. and let it hang several days until the fat penetrates the skin.

Next, make a solution of

5 gallons water
1 pound strong laundry detergent (Borax)

Soak the hide in this for several days. Not having laundry detergent, the Indians mashed up the deer brains and rubbed them into the hide. They said each deer had the exact amount of brains necessary to cure the hide. When you remove it from the solution, wash it carefully in fresh water and get on your sweat suit because you're going to need it for the next step.

Softening the Skin

You must twist and pull the moist skin over the edge of a pole or something until it is VELVETY soft. A clothesline pole may be adequate for this but the Indians used a sharp-edged stick driven firmly into the ground. If you can invent any shortcuts for this, let me know, for it takes time and muscle, but don't stint on this step because the quality of your buckskin depends on this.

Smoking the Hide

You must smoke it to close the pores. It is said that if this done properly, the buckskin can get wet or even be washed and it will remain soft. The Indians

Chapter Three

used to wrap it in a cone shape under which a tiny, smoky fire had been built. However you arrange it, take care that no flames or heat get near it, or it will be ruined. Probably the easiest way is to put it on an oven rack suspended about four feet over a small, smoky fire.

TO MAKE RAWHIDE

First, scrape all of the flesh from the inside of the skin. If you have let the hide dry out, you might have to moisten it with water first.

Next, make a solution of:

5 gallons of water
1 quart of wood ashes (optional)
1 quart of hydrated lime

Soak the hide in this solution for several days, making sure all parts are covered at all times. Remove it from the bath and scrape both sides perfectly clean, taking care not to pierce the skin. Set up a frame in a shady spot and stretch the skin on the frame, stretching as tightly as possible. Let it dry thoroughly.

RAWHIDE LACES

To make rawhide laces, rub the dried skin with mineral oil, neat's-foot oil, etc., cut the rawhide into thin strips and soften by pulling them back and forth over a sturdy post.

WINDOW GLASS REPLACEMENT

Take a thoroughly clean rawhide skin and rub it with a mixture of the whites of eggs and honey. Do this while it is still stretched on the frame, but after it is thoroughly dry. Keep rubbing the honey and egg

Big Game

mixture into the rawhide until it is translucent.

GUN RACKS FROM THE LEGS AND FEET

Make a mixture of water and moth flakes and soak the legs and feet in this until you can bend the ankles into position and dry. Saw the legs off evenly and plug with wood.

HARD HIDE CURING

If you want a very simple curing process to preserve the hide for a rug or a wall hanging, this can suffice. My taxidermist consultant, Mr. Dick Sutton, does not admire or approve of this method because it does not result in a fine, soft, well-preserved hide, but some hunters around here do this because it is fast and adequate for their purposes.

First, scrape all flesh from the inside of the skin, taking care not to pierce it. After it is scraped clean, apply uniodized salt heavily to the flesh side, rubbing it in. Fold it, flesh side to flesh side, roll it up and prop it up in an elevated position for 24 hours so the blood and bodily fluids will drain from it. After 24 hours, unroll it, scrape it carefully and repeat the salt and draining treatment.

After you have repeated this procedure three times, stretch it on a frame as directed under RAWHIDE and allow it to dry thoroughly.

Big Game Delicacies
Chapter 4

Kidneys

CLEANING AND PRETREATING

First, trim off all of the fat, split the kidneys down the middle and trim out the white center and the tubes. Now wash them, skin them and put to soak for at least several hours in salt water. (1 teaspoon of salt to 1 quart of water.) My mother always soaked them overnight and changed the water several times.

BROILED KIDNEYS

Prepare kidneys by the preceding rule. Remove them from the salt water and dry them with paper towels. Make the following marinade. Mix:

1/8 cup vinegar
3/8 cup oil
1 clove peeled garlic crushed by a fork with 1/4 teaspoon of salt
Pepper and herbs to taste

Soak the prepared kidneys in the marinade for at

Big Game

least three hours or overnight. This step tenderizes the kidneys, so overnight is better. Broil them under moderate heat for 10 to 15 minutes, brushing them with the marinade and turning them midway. They are delicious served with broiled bacon, mushrooms and halved tomatoes, which may be added to the broiling pan when you turn the kidneys after the first 5 minutes. Watch carefully, this is not something you can toss in the oven and walk away from, but since the whole broiling process takes about 10 minutes this should not be too great a strain. It is truly a feast.

PAN FRIED KIDNEYS

Clean and pretreat the kidneys as described above. Remove them from the soaking water and preboil them for 5 minutes in clean, lightly salted water. Do not overcook or you will toughen them. Drain them and pat them dry. Slice them crosswise into very thin slices and saute them for about 5 minutes in melted butter, stirring gently. Taste (remember you have soaked and precooked them in salt water so you have to be very careful about oversalting), toss on buttered toast, and serve.

Tongue

Cut the tongue out from as far back as it is possible. Remember that the same principle applies with the tongue as with the rest of the animal -- the younger the animal, the more tender.

BOILED TONGUE

Wash the tongue carefully. Put in pot with 1 chopped onion, 1 chopped carrot, 1 chopped celery, 1 tea-

Chapter Four

spoon Italian seasoning, 2 teaspoons salt and 3 quarts of water. Bring it to a boil and let it boil about 10 minutes, then remove the scum. Reduce heat and simmer until tender, which will be from 3 to 5 hours, depending on the size of the tongue and the age of the animal. When it's fork tender, cool it in the stock. Remove it and skin it. Remove fat and hard portions on the throat end. Slice it thinly against the grain and serve with horseradish sauce.

BRAISED TONGUE

Plunge the tongue into boiling water for 5 minutes, remove and skin. Brown 2 large sliced onions in 2 tablespoons oil and 2 tablespoons butter. Push to one side and brown the skinned tongue on all sides. Lightly salt tongue all over. Add 1 can beef bouillon and 1 can water, 1 teaspoon Italian seasoning, 1 bay leaf and 1/4 cup wine. Put in 325° F. oven for 3 to 5 hours, depending on the size of the tongue and the age of the animal, until fork tender. Slice against the grain and serve with pan drippings.

BREADED SLICED TONGUE

Slice boiled or braised tongue into 1/4 inch thick slices. Dip into beaten egg, then into seasoned bread crumbs. Fry gently in butter until golden brown.
Serve with Sour Cream Sauce, Devil Sauce or Cheese Sauce. (See Index).

Liver

CLEANING AND FREEZING

Trim the membranes and the tubes from the liver

Big Game

and wash it. Cool and refrigerate the liver as soon as possible and eat it within two or three days. If you cannot eat it soon, freeze it. When it is almost frozen, cut it into slices 1/2 inch thick and wrap it with Saran Wrap. Separate the slices so it does not freeze into a large lump. Bear liver must be braised or oven baked.

BRAISED LIVER (For an older animal)

Prepare liver as directed above. Melt 1/4 cup butter in a kettle. Lightly salt and pepper sliced liver and dredge with flour. Gently sizzle in butter until lightly browned on both sides. Remove from pan. Add to the kettle, 1 can tiny whole carrots and 1 can tiny whole onions, including the juices from both. Lay browned slices of liver on top of vegetables. Put in 350° F. oven for 1 to 2 hours or until fork tender.

LIVER SAUTEED WITH BACON (From a young animal)

Clean and slice liver as directed above. Fry 4 to 6 slices of bacon and drain on a paper towel. Lay liver in the bacon fat and gently sizzle for about 5 minutes on each side, or until it is browned on the outside but still faintly pink on the inside. Serve with crumbled bacon over the top.

LIVER SPREAD

Delicious! Clean liver as directed above. Saute in butter or margarine 1 pound cleaned liver and 1 pound cleaned, fresh mushrooms. Put both through a meat chopper, using a fine blade. Put it in the top of a double boiler, over boiling water, and add 1/8 cup white wine and 1/8 cup cream. Salt and pepper to taste. When hot, beat vigorously and serve on hot buttered toast.

Chapter Four

BRAISED LIVER WITH SOUR CREAM GRAVY

Simmer the liver in salted water for 10 minutes. Drain. Clean the liver, removing the tubes, membrane and skin. Cover with 1 1/2 cups wine, 1/2 cup oil, 1 teaspoon Italian seasoning or thyme, 1 clove garlic mashed with salt. Marinate overnight turning occasionally. Remove the liver, dry and brown quickly on all sides in butter or margarine. Put it in an oiled casserole dish, add marinade, COVER and roast in $325°$ F. oven for 1 to 2 hours, until tender, turning several times. Put the liver on a hot platter, pour off fat from pan drippings and add 1 cup sour cream. Stir, heat and taste for seasoning but do not let it boil. Serve with the liver, to ladle over it.

Heart

CLEANING

Soak the heart in cold, salted water to which 4 tablespoons vinegar has been added for one hour or overnight. Trim away fat, veins and hard parts. This will make a clean pocket within for stuffing.

ROAST, STUFFED HEART

Stuffing: Lightly brown 1/2 pound sausage meat, 1/4 cup chopped onions, 1/4 cup chopped celery. Add 2 cups bread crumbs and salt and pepper to taste. Stuff heart and close top with skewers. Brown it lightly in a casserole dish, tossing to brown all sides. Add 1 1/2 cups chicken broth and 1/4 cup red wine. COVER and bake for 2 hours, turning occasionally. Serve sliced with broth sprinkled over.

Big Game

SAUTEED HEART (Very young animals only)

Prepare heart as directed above in cleaning. Wash and slice the heart in very thin slices. Crush 1 clove garlic with 1/2 teaspoon salt and brown in 4 tablespoons oil. Push the garlic to one side and add the dried heart slices. Brown them well, 5 minutes on one side and 5 minutes on the other. Remove to a hot platter. Add 1 heaping tablespoon frozen lemonade mixture to the pan drippings, stir for 30 seconds over heat and pour over the heart slices. Serve.

Brains

Drop the brains into boiling water to which has been added 1/2 sliced lemon, 1 1/2 teaspoon salt, and 1/2 teaspoon pepper. Simmer gently for 15 minutes. Drain, cool, skin and clean. Saute (gently fry) them in gently sizzling butter or margarine, 8 minutes on one side and 8 minutes on the other. Put on a warm platter. Add a little more butter to the drippings and gently brown, pour over the brains and serve with lemon wedges.

The Indians used the brains to make buckskin. See directions under "Buckskin".

Big Game Corned

BIG GAME CORNED

20-30 pounds meat, preferably boned and cut into 3-4 pound pieces
3 gallons water
3 pounds salt (3 to 4 cups)

1 cup sugar
1 tablespoon baking soda
1 ounce sodium nitrite (get in drug store) (optional)
4 teaspoons freshly ground black pepper
3 teaspoons Italian seasoning or thyme
3 tablespoons mixed pickling spice
1 full head garlic, mashed with 1 tablespoon salt

If you can find a corner of your basement which stays around 40 degrees F., fine. If you can't find such a cool place, add one pound of salt for every 15 degrees higher. The meat remains in the liquid for 15 days. Turn it every five days. If the brine starts to get gummy or stringy, remove the meat and wash it. Discard the brine, clean and sterilize the container and refill with new brine. It can be kept in good brine for 4-6 weeks, or remove the meat from the liquid and freeze until time to use. To cook, place in a deep pot and cover with clear water. Bring to a boil and boil five minutes. Pour off the water. Add fresh water to cover and simmer for about 5 hours, until tender. Serve with horseradish sauce.

SIMPLE BIG GAME CORNED MEAT (For smaller amounts)

Stir together thoroughly:

2 quarts water
1 cup salt
1 tablespoon Italian seasoning
1 clove garlic, crushed with salt
2 teaspoons mixed pickle spice
1/4 teaspoon saltpeter (optional)
2 teaspoons pepper

Add 6 pounds BONED meat. Cover it with a plate and put a heavy weight on it. Leave the meat in the

Big Game

brine for 48 hours or more. Remove from brine, wash and tie to keep in shape. Place it in cold water to cover. Bring it to the boiling point, remove the scum, cover it and simmer for 4 to 5 hours. Skim at intervals. Let it cool in broth. Serve it with any horseradish sauce. You can also follow any cookbook recipe such as corned beef and cabbage, etc.

Big Game Mincemeat

Bake 60 minutes at 350 degrees, 4 or 5 pounds of meat, all fat trimmed off. You can simmer it, covered with water, until tender, but I prefer the roasted taste. Chop the meat finely with 2 pounds beef or pork fat. (Wild game fat is often strong tasting and can ruin the taste of the meat.) Mix the finely chopped meat and fat with:

10 pounds finely chopped, tart apples
4 pounds currants, if available
6 pounds raisins
1 pound citron or candied fruit (chopped)
10 cups brown sugar (moore if needed to taste)
5 teaspoons nutmeg
3 tablespoons allspice
4 tablespoons cinnamon
1 teaspoon ginger
2 teaspoons cloves
1 1/2 tablespoons salt
6 finely chopped whole oranges
2 cups vinegar
10 cups cider

Simmer for 1 1/2 hours. Correct seasoning. If you like rum, sherry, brandy or whiskey in your mincemeat, add it now to your taste. If you are a teetotaler but like the taste, add rum or sherry extract.

You can store the mincemeat in the refrigerator for several weeks, in the freezer for months, or immediately pack into hot jars, seal and process in pressure canner for 50 minutes for pints and 70 minutes for quarts at 15 pounds pressure.

Big Game Spareribs

Well cooked spareribs are brown and tender; therefore, you must start off with high heat until they are browned, then cover and roast at a low heat until they are very done.

STUFFED SPARERIBS

Make a dressing as follows. Mix:

1 1/2 cup bread crumbs or diced bread
1/2 cup chopped onion
1/4 cup melted butter or margarine
Salt and pepper to taste
Italian seasoning, poultry seasoning, dried sage or parsley to taste

Spread the inside of one piece of the spareribs with the dressing, and cover it with the other piece and tie together. Salt and pepper both sides. Place it in a roasting pan and into a preheated 450 degree F. oven for 15 or 20 minutes, until it is nicely browned. Turn the oven back to 300 degrees F., put 1 cup of water into the pan, COVER and bake for 1 hour. Test for tenderness. It may be slowly baked for another hour if needed.

OVEN BARBECUED SPARERIBS

Cut the spareribs into serving sized pieces and brown them on each side under the broiler or in a very hot (500 degree F.) oven. Cover them with your favorite barbecue sauce, or follow the directions for Devil Barbecue Sauce under Sauces. COVER the pan and bake in a very slow oven (250 degrees F.) for two to three hours, until perfectly tender when pierced with a fork.

CHARCOAL BARBECUED SPARERIBS

Bring to a boil and immediately remove from heat the Devil Barbecue Sauce listed under Sauces. You may have to double or triple the quantity, depending on the amount of ribs you are preparing. Spread the ribs out in a large roaster and cover with the Devil Sauce. Let them soak in the sauce for several hours or overnight. Remove them from the sauce, taking care that as much of the sauce as possible clings to the ribs, and place them over glowing charcoal, high above the heat. Grill very slowly, turning them and brushing them with as much of the marinade as possible, until they are very tender to the fork. Yummmmmmm!

Big Game Sausage

6 to 8 pounds ground game
6 to 8 pounds ground pork
1 tablespoon saltpeter (drugstore) (optional)
1 tablespoon garlic powder
2 tablespoons salt
1 tablespoon pepper
1 1/2 tablespoons Italian seasoning, crushed between fingers

Chapter Four

Mix together thoroughly. Make a tiny ball and fry it out, then taste for seasoning. (Never taste raw pork or game.) When it tastes good, pack in sausage bags or casings and follow directions from index for 12 to 24 hours of smoking. Freeze if not used immediately.

Big Game Recipes

Chapter 5

All About Venison

VENISON IS PROPERLY DEFINED AS THE FLESH OF A DEER OR SIMILAR ANIMAL. When I refer to venison in this book I mean deer, elk, moose, etc. All skinning, cleaning and cooking directions for large game are interchangeable except for the bear and the wild boar, who belong to the pig family when meat treatment and recipes are concerned.

Any of your favorite beef recipes may be used for venison and any of your favorite pork recipes may be used for the bear and wild boar. Remember that the fat in most wild animals is very strong tasting and should be trimmed off. Beef and pork fat should be substituted either by larding (making slits in the meat with the tip of a sharp knife and stuffing in fatty pieces such as salt pork, bacon, etc.), or by tying the fatty strips around the piece of meat.

The wild animal is leaner because he gets a lot more exercise than domestic animals. Remember, he has to fend for himself. And as far as being clean, remember that no wild animal has to spend most of his life in

Chapter Five

a barnyard with a lot of other animals.

You will have to try to judge the age of the animal by his size, how much his teeth are worn, etc. If he's bigger and older, chances are he's tougher, and you should barbecue, marinate, braise or stew him, or at least add tenderizer to the meat BEFORE you freeze it. Canning is also great for tougher animals as it's a natural tenderizer.

MARINADE

A marinade is used to tenderize and flavor wild game. An all-purpose mixture follows. Feel free to add any of your favorite herbs. Taste it until it tastes good to you, then soak your meat in it as instructed, at least 24 hours.

1 cup wine OR 1/2 cup lemon juice OR 2 cups tomato juice.
   (This acid ingredient is to tenderize)
3/4 cup oil (to bind the marinade and make it cling to the meat)
2 teaspoons of tenderizer (optional, just safety)
1 teaspoon salt
1/2 cup chopped onion
1 clove garlic, peeled and crushed with a fork with a little salt to liquefy
1 teaspoon Italian seasoning or any herbs you love to use

Antelope

PRONGHORN

The pronghorn is called the "American antelope", but it is not a true antelope. It has no close relatives

Big Game

and has changed little in two million years. It is gutted, skinned and processed like a deer, so please consult the big game directions. Make sure you know about dressing your antelope BEFORE you go hunting and you will be rewarded with a lower grocery bill and happy family eaters. Remember, the antelope eats sage so it takes well to wine, onions and bacon. It does not need herbs.

ANTELOPE SKINNING, BUTCHERING, TANNING, BUCKSKIN, RAWHIDE, CANNING, DRYING AND SMOKING ARE AT THE BEGINNING OF THE BOOK.

ANTELOPE LIVER, KIDNEYS, TONGUE, BRAINS, HEART, MINCEMEAT AND SAUSAGE ARE AT THE BEGINNING OF THE BOOK.

ANTELOPE ROAST

Make small slits in the roast at two to three inch intervals and insert bacon or salt pork and onion salt. Rub generously with oil, then cover with onion salt and pepper and thin strips of bacon or salt pork. Put in a roasting pan and roast it in a $450°$ F. oven for 15 minutes per pound (1 hour for 4 pound roast). Add 1/4 cup wine to pan drippings and stir and swirl for one minute. Pour over roast or serve with it as desired.

ANTELOPE STEAKS WITH PORT WINE AND CURRANT JELLY

Have steaks cut 3/4 inch thick and marinate them overnight in port wine, to which has been added one chopped onion. Turn several times. Remove from wine and dry. Put 4 tablespoons oil in a very hot, heavy frying pan and sauté (gently fry) quickly over high heat for 4 minutes on each side. Put on a hot platter. Pour in the port wine marinade, first removing onions. Add

Chapter Five

1/4 cup currant jelly and stir and swirl until heated and smooth. Pour over steaks and serve.

ANTELOPE SHISH KEBOB

Make marinade of 1/4 cup oil, juice of 2 to 3 lemons, 1 tsp. onion salt, 2 teaspoons onion juice, 1 teaspoon curry powder (more if you like it hotter), 1 clove garlic mashed with salt. Cut antelope in two inch cubes and marinate overnight, stirring and turning frequently. Thread on skewers, alternating with two inch pieces of tomato, green pepper, small onions, etc. Broil until browned lightly on all sides, basting often with marinade.

Elk

My husband's grandfather, Alexander Billmeyer of Washingtonville, Pennsylvania, was famous for his elk park which he maintained for his own pleasure and for anyone who cared to come. Thousands came. His biggest and most favorite was Jumbo, and we have a picture of him pulling a cart. But many of them were dangerous, even after being in the park for many years. If you are lucky enough to bag an elk, follow the directions at the beginning of the book for cleaning and caring for big game, and you'll have great eating for months.

ELK SKINNING, BUTCHERING, TANNING, BUCKSKIN, RAWHIDE, CANNING, DRYING, AND SMOKING ARE AT THE BEGINNING OF THE BOOK.

ELK LIVER, KIDNEYS, TONGUE, BRAINS, HEART, MINCEMEAT AND SAUSAGE ARE AT THE BEGINNING OF THE BOOK.

Big Game

ELK SWISS STEAK

Have meat prepared as described in the beginning of the book. Lightly pepper and salt steak, then pound in the flour with a heavy knife or the edge of a heavy plate. Pound in as much on both sides as the steaks will hold. Cut into serving pieces and quickly brown on both sides in butter or margarine. Pour in 1/8 cup sherry and 1 cup chicken broth. COVER and bake in 350° F. oven for 1 to 1 1/2 hours or until fork tender. Put steak on a warm platter. Add 1 cup chicken broth to the pan drippings. Then combine 1 1/2 tablespoons butter with 1 1/2 tablespoons flour and stir into the broth. Stir and cook until thick, smooth and bubbling. Correct seasoning. Pour over steak and serve with buttered rice with herbs.

BUTTERED RICE WITH HERBS

This is the only way to cook fluffy, well done rice. Fill your largest kettle with water to which 1 tablespoon salt has been added and bring it to a boil. Add 2 cups raw rice, bring it to a boil and adjust the heat so it keeps in a slow, rolling boil. Boil for about 40 minutes, or until a grain tested between the teeth is done. Drain and wash carefully with hot water. I freeze what I am not going to use immmediately and just toss it in butter when I want to serve it.

Melt 1/2 cup butter or margarine in a saucepan, add 2 cups cooked rice, 1/2 teaspoon Italian seasoning or thyme and salt and pepper to taste. Toss the rice in the gently sizzling butter for 4 minutes, or until hot through and gently coated with butter. Serve.

SWEET AND SOUR ELK RIBS
(For 4 to 5 pounds of ribs)
Combine 1/3 cup oil, 1/2 cup soy sauce, 1/3 cup

catsup, juice of 2 lemons, 1/3 cup brown sugar, 1 teaspoon garlic or onion salt, 1 clove garlic mashed with 1 teaspoon salt, and 1/2 teaspoon pepper. Grease a roasting pan, add ribs in a single layer and pour sauce over the top. COVER and bake at 350° F. for 1 1/4 hours, turning several times. UNCOVER and bake until brown and fork tender. Serve with french fries and creamed cabbage.

FOIL ROASTED ELK

Lightly salt and pepper roast on both sides and place on a large piece of foil. Sprinkle over the top 1/4 cup sherry or port wine or lemon juice, then sprinkle 1 envelope dry onion soup mixture. Seal and roast in a roasting pan for 2 to 3 hours at 375° F. It is is done when it is fork tender.

Deer

DEER, MULE DEER, COLUMBIAN BLACK TAILED DEER, VIRGINIA WHITE TAILED DEER, KEY DEER, WHITE TAILED DEER

DEER SKINNING, BUTCHERING, TANNING, BUCKSKIN, RAWHIDE, CANNING, DRYING, AND SMOKING ARE AT THE BEGINNING OF THE BOOK.

DEER LIVER, KIDNEYS, TONGUE, BRAINS, HEART, MINCEMEAT AND SAUSAGE ARE AT THE BEGINNING OF THE BOOK.

DEER MEAT LOAF

Superb! In a blender put 2 whole eggs, 1 large onion, quartered, and 1/8 cup sherry (more or less or none, depending on your convictions). Run on liquify

Big Game

for 5 seconds. Pour into large mixing bowl. Add 1 pound venison hamburger, 1/3 pound ground pork or sausage meat, 1 teaspoon salt, 1/4 teaspoon pepper, 1/2 teaspoon poultry seasoning and 1 cup bread crumbs. Mix thoroughly and fry out 1 teaspoon of the mixture to taste for seasoning. Correct if necessary. Put in a buttered loaf pan which has been lined with thin strips of salt pork or bacon. Bake at $375°$ F. for 1 hour. Remove to a warm platter and take off strips of salt pork. Degrease pan drippings, strain, pour over loaf, and serve.

PAN BROILED DEER STEAKS
(See cleaning directions in Chapter One)

Have steaks cut 3/4 inch thick. Lightly sprinkle with salt and pepper and place them in the following marinade or use the big game marinade listed at the beginning of this cooking section.

1/4 cup red wine
1/8 cup gin
1/4 cup oil
1 teaspoon Italian seasoning or thyme
1 clove garlic
1 sliced onion

Marinate the steaks for 24 to 48 hours, turning frequently. Remove them and pat them dry. Heat 3 tablespoons oil in a heavy frying pan and sauté (gently fry) steaks for 3 minutes for each side over high heat. (If you want them more well done, increase the cooking time slightly.) Put steaks on a hot platter. Strain marinade into pan drippings and boil down to half the amount over high heat. Pour over steaks and serve.

Chapter Five

DEER CHOPS STROGANOFF

See cleaning directions at the beginning of chapter one. Cover the chops with the marinade described above in "Pan Broiled Steaks". Marinate them for 24 hours, turning several times. Remove and dry. Sauté (gently fry) the chops in a heavy skillet in 4 tablespoons oil or crisco for 3 to 4 minutes on each side. Put on a hot platter. Strain the marinade into the pan drippings and boil down to half over high heat. Stir and scrape, add 1 cup sour cream then heat to the boiling point. Remove from heat and pour over the chops. Serve with fried bread.

FRIED BREAD

Trim the edges off bread and cut diagonally. Fry gently in butter until lightly brown on both sides. Serve hot.

Buffalo

BISON

At one time there were only about 500 buffalo left in the United States. After being declared an endangered species, they gradually built up again. Buffalo meat is lean and must be larded (fat added), otherwise it may be prepared with any beef recipe.

BUFFALO SKINNING, BUTCHERING, TANNING, BUCKSKIN, RAWHIDE, CANNING, DRYING, AND SMOKING ARE AT THE BEGINNING OF THE BOOK.

BUFFALO LIVER, KIDNEYS, TONGUE, BRAINS, HEART, MINCEMEAT AND SAUSAGE ARE AT THE BEGINNING OF THE BOOK.

Big Game

BUFFALO BRAISED IN PORT

Marinade:

1 1/2 cups port wine or 1/2 cup lemon juice
1/4 cup vinegar
1/4 cup soy sauce
2 tablespoons brown sugar
1 bay leaf
1 teaspoon Italian seasoning or thyme
1 sliced onion
1 clove garlic mashed with salt

Mix together and pour over a 3 to 4 pound buffalo steak, filet or roast. COVER and keep in the refrigerator for 24 to 48 hours, turning twice a day. Remove the meat and wipe dry. Lightly salt, pepper and dredge with flour. In a roasting pan, heat 1/4 cup of butter, margarine, or oil and brown both sides of the meat using high heat. Strain the marinade and add it to the pan. Cover the top of the roast with thinly sliced onions, then with thinly sliced salt pork or bacon. Put in a 325° F. oven and roast for 2 to 3 hours, until it is fork tender, and brown. Baste frequently and turn once during roasting. Serve with a tart meat accompaniment (chili sauce, mint jelly, etc.).

BROILED BUFFALO STEAKS (must be young, tender buffalo)

Have the steaks cut 3/4 to 1 inch thick. Sprinkle with tenderizer. Place them on a buttered broiler rack, and put them as close to the heat as possible, searing the juices in on both sides. Test them for desired doneness. Place 2 inches from the heat and broil to desired doneness, basting several times with melted butter. Pour more melted butter over and serve. If your steaks are frozen, never thaw them before cooking. Follow the directions given above, allowing the extra time needed since they are frozen.

BARBECUED BUFFALO STEAKS

Marinade:

Mix 1 cup oil, 1/2 cup red wine or 1/4 cup vinegar or lemon juice, 2 garlic cloves crushed in 1 teaspoon salt, 1 teaspoon pepper, 1 small chopped onion, 1 teaspoon Italian seasoning or thyme, and 1 large bay leaf in glass bowl. Add steaks and let them soak for 24 to 48 hours. Turn every 12 hours. Place on broiler rack as close to the heat as possible, searing in the juices on both sides. Place 2 to 3 inches away from the flame and broil to desired doneness, basting often with marinade. Serve on hot platters.

Goat

MOUNTAIN GOAT, ROCKY MOUNTAIN GOAT

This animal looks like a goat, but it is more closely related to the antelope. Its average weight is 200 pounds and it must be gutted, skinned, and processed as directed at the beginning of the book. When it is young, it can be cooked like pig or lamb. When it is older, it must be marinated and/or larded to become tender.

GOAT SKINNING, BUTCHERING, TANNING, BUCKSKIN, RAWHIDE, CANNING, DRYING, AND SMOKING ARE AT THE BEGINNING OF THE BOOK.

GOAT LIVER, KIDNEYS, TONGUE, BRAINS, HEART, MINCEMEAT AND SAUSAGE ARE AT THE BEGINNING OF THE BOOK.

Big Game

MOUNTAIN GOAT KEBABS (For a young animal)

Cut three pounds lean young goat meat in 1 inch cubes. Mix 1/2 cup oil, 1/2 cup soy sauce, 1 crushed garlic clove and 1 teaspoon ground ginger in a glass bowl. Stir in goat cubes and marinate 2 hours to 24 hours, stirring every 6 hours or so. String on skewers alternately with cubes of pineapple. Broil until brown on all sides, brushing liberally with the marinade.

MOUNTAIN GOAT ROAST (Older animal)

Lard 4 to 5 pound roast with garlic slivers, salt, and bacon or salt pork. (Make slits at three inch intervals with tip of sharp knife and insert salt, garlic clove sliver and fat meat.) Rub outside with garlic powder and lay fat meat slices over the top. Put in covered roasting pan to which has been added 1 can beef bouillon and 1 can of water. Cook at 325° F. for 4 to 5 hours or until tender and brown. Serve with buttered, herbed rice.

Moose

The moose is the largest animal of the deer family. They can weigh up to 850 pounds. If you shoot a moose, you will need a very large freezer!

MOOSE SKINNING, BUTCHERING, TANNING, BUCKSKIN, RAWHIDE, CANNING, DRYING AND SMOKING ARE AT THE BEGINNING OF THE BOOK.

MOOSE LIVER, KIDNEYS, TONGUE, BRAINS, HEART, MINCEMEAT AND SAUSAGE ARE AT THE BEGINNING OF THE BOOK.

Remember that you or the butcher must hang the moose meat for two to four weeks before butchering it.

Also, it is almost always necessary to marinate the meat before cooking.

MOOSE ROAST WITH CHESTNUTS AND CREAM

Make sure the skin and sinews are removed from a 5 pound moose roast. (If it is larger, increase the marinade and roasting time.) Into a glass or enameled bowl, mix 2 cups wine or 1/2 cup lemon juice, 1 teaspoon Italian seasoning, 1/2 teaspoon pepper, 1/2 teaspoon salt, 2 onions and 1 clove garlic liquefied with salt. Lard the roast with bacon or salt pork. (At three inch intervals, insert tip of sharp knife and poke in garlic salt and bacon or salt pork.) Leave covered, in refrigerator for 48 hours, turning every 12 hours. Drain and dry the roast and put in an oiled roasting pan to which has been added the onions and garlic clove from the marinade. Roast at 325° F. for 1 1/2 hours, raising the heat to 425° F. for the last 15 minutes to brown. Remove the roast to a hot platter and add the marinade to the juices. Boil at high heat for two minutes, turn off heat and add 1/4 to 1/2 cup cream and 1/2 cup sliced chestnuts. Season to taste and serve a little over each slice of meat.

MOOSE SAUSAGE

Combine 4 pounds ground moose meat with 4 to 5 pounds fatty pork. Make sure you include all the pork fat. If necessary, add 1/2 pound ground bacon or salt pork. Mix it with 1 teaspoon salt, 1 teaspoon pepper, 1 teaspoon garlic powder, and 1 teaspoon Italian seasoning. Make a small ball of mixture and fry, then taste for seasoning. (Never taste uncooked pork mixture.) Correct seasoning and make into sausage patties or stuff into sausage casings. If not used immediately, freeze.

Big Game

Sheep

ROCKY MOUNTAIN SHEEP, BIGHORN, DALL SHEEP, STONE SHEEP, ARIZONA DESERT BIGHORN SHEEP

The mountain sheep is said to be the most promiscuous of the big game animals. It is said he constantly searches for receptive females whom he pursues until he is successful. Sound familiar?

These animals belong to the cattle family and may be processed and cooked like deer. They should be gutted and skinned as quickly as possible and hung so air can circulate around them freely, dissipating body heat.

SHEEP SKINNING, BUTCHERING, TANNING, BUCKSKIN, RAWHIDE, CANNING, DRYING AND SMOKING ARE AT THE BEGINNING OF THE BOOK.

SHEEP LIVER, KIDNEYS, TONGUE, BRAINS, HEART, MINCEMEAT AND SAUSAGE ARE AT THE BEGINNING OF THE BOOK.

ROCKY MOUNTAIN BIGHORN SHEEP ROAST

For a 5 pound roast, mix 1 cup vinegar, 1 cup water, 1 tablespoon meat tenderizer, 1 tablespoon salt, 1 tablespoon pepper, 1 large sliced onion and 1 teaspoon Italian seasoning in a deep glass bowl. Add the roast and marinate from 2 hours to 24 hours. Pour liquid off, pour 1 cup port wine or 1 cup beef broth and 1 package dry onion soup in roasting pan and add roast. Cover and roast 20 minutes at $400°$ F. then 1 1/2 hours at $325°$ F. or UNTIL FORK TENDER. Add more liquid if necessary. (Canned, diluted beef or chicken broth is adequate.)

YOUNG BIGHORN SHEEP ROAST
(For a very young, tender sheep.)

Chapter Five

Lard a 3 to 5 pound roast with bacon or salt pork. (Insert point of sharp knife every three inches and poke in garlic salt and a piece of bacon or salt pork.) Put garlic salt and pepper on the outside and dredge it with flour. Put it in a 400° F. oven for 30 minutes, uncovered, then cover it and roast it at 325° F. until fork tender, about 2 hours. Serve with the horseradish sauce listed at the end of this chapter.

Bear

BLACK BEAR, GRIZZLEY BEAR, KODIAK BEAR, ALASKAN BROWN BEAR

Mr. Don Kepler of Pine Grove Mills, Pennsylvania, has killed 11 bear as of this writing. He has become famous for giving the rendered bear fat to people suffering from arthritis, injured joints, and other ailments. I had a friend who burned the hair off the top of her head. Her hairdresser, in desperation, put bear grease on and told her to leave it on overnight. She smelled like a wet bear, but it worked! She claimed it restored her hair. She has since recommended it to other women whose hair is falling out and it has never failed to improve it. Therefore, I am including Mr. Kepler's method of rendering bear fat.

A male bear in the mating season, like a boar hog, is not fit to eat. Anyone who would kill a nursing mother bear would be a rotten person, so I'm sure no one reading this book will fall under that category. A young male bear, however, is delicious to eat.

BEAR SKINNING, BUTCHERING, TANNING, BEARSKIN, RAWHIDE, CANNING, DRYING, AND SMOKING ARE AT THE BEGINNING OF THE BOOK.

Big Game

SKINNING THE BEAR

Follow the standard directions for large game specified previously except carefully trim off the fat or it will give the meat a strong taste. Save it and render it, following the directions given. The neck and hindquarters are muscular and will probably be stringy and tough. They are best trimmed out and ground into hamburger with beef suet added. If you want to roast them, braise them with liquid added, otherwise they will be tough.

The bear loves sweets - berries, honey, etc. make up a large part of his diet - so his meat is rich and sweet. He is a big, tough animal and must be aged as instructed previously, also his meat must be marinated for tenderizing.

BEAR MARINADE

1 cup wine OR 1/2 cup lemon juice OR 2 cups tomato juice (this acid ingredient is the tenderizing agent)
3/4 cup oil (to bind the marinade and make it cling to the meat.)
2 teaspoons tenderizer, if possible (one can't be too careful about tenderizing a bear)
1 teaspoon salt
Pepper and herbs to taste - use your favorites. I like Italian Seasoning and Parsley. Many people like cloves and allspice with the rich meat of bear. Onions and garlic are a great addition too.

You can double or triple this amount if needed. Marinate the bear meat 1 to 5 days, depending on the size of the pieces and the amount of time you can wait to try him.

BEAR LIVER, KIDNEYS, TONGUE, BRAINS, HEART,

Chapter Five

MINCEMEAT AND SAUSAGE ARE AT THE BEGINNING OF THE BOOK.

BEAR FAT RENDERING (From Mr. Don Kepler, Pine Grove Mills, Pa.)

Fill a dishpan half full of water and bring it to a boil. Set in the boiling water a smaller pan containing the fat, sliced. Keep the water slowly boiling and the fat will melt. After it melts, pour it through a cloth and put it into a jar and seal. It keeps for years and is an old remedy for joint injury, arthritis, cuts or hair restoration.

ROAST LOIN OF BEAR

Lard a 5 to 8 pound loin by sticking the point of a small knife in the meat, then stuff in strips of salt pork or bacon and garlic salt. Do this at 2 to 3 inch intervals. Marinate the meat for 3 to 5 days, covered and in the refrigerator in the following marinade:

Mix 3 cups wine (optional), 1/2 cup vinegar, 1 cup oil, 1 cup chopped celery, 2 cloves garlic mashed with salt, 3 chopped onions, 3 chopped carrots, 3 bay leaves, 1 teaspoon Italian seasoning or tarragon, 2 teaspoons salt and 1 teaspoon pepper. Bring it to a boil and cook, taste for seasoning, then use to cover the meat in an enameled or earthenware bowl. Turn the meat twice a day. Strain the marinade and boil it down to 2 cups. Put the vegetables from the marinade in the bottom of a roasting pan and set the meat on top of them. Roast at $425°$ F. for 20 minutes. Reduce the heat to $350°$ F. and roast for 1 1/2 to 2 hours, until tender, basting frequently. Put the meat on a warm platter, add the marinade liquid to the pan drippings and simmer, stirring and scraping. Taste for seasoning, pour over roast bear and serve.

Big Game

BEAR STEW

If you are not sure of the age of your bear, this is a safe bet. Cut the bear into 2 inch cubes, salt and pepper lightly and toss in flour. Brown in butter or margarine, shaking and turning the meat so it browns all around. Add 1 cup wine, 1 cup chicken broth, 1 garlic clove mashed with salt, 1 bay leaf and 1 teaspoon Italian seasoning or thyme. Bring to a boil and put in a $325°$ F. oven for 3 to 4 hours, until tender. One-half hour before serving, add 1 can tiny whole carrots and 1 can tiny whole onions. Taste for seasoning and serve with hot bread and salad.

BROILED BEAR STEAK

Marinate steaks for two days in the following marinade, turning frequently: 2 cups wine, 1 cup oil, 1/2 cup vinegar, 2 bay leaves, 1 teaspoon Italian seasoning and 1 garlic clove mashed with salt. Remove the steaks from the marinade, dry and put 3 inches from the broiler. Broil 6 to 8 minutes on each side, depending on the size of the steak. Serve with french fries and horseradish.

Javelina or Wild Pig

WILD BOAR, COLLARD PECCARY, JAVELINA OR MUSK HOG

The standard field dressing instructions at the beginning of this book apply, EXCEPT in the middle of the back, towards the rear, is a musk gland. If this was damaged by the bullet the meat is inedible. If not, proceed with the standard gutting instructions. Next, THE

Chapter Five

ANIMAL MUST BE SKINNED OUT AT ONCE, MAKING SURE NOT TO PIERCE THE MUSK GLAND. REMOVE THE GLAND, CUTTING THE MEAT AROUND IT TO ENSURE IT IS NOT PIERCED. WASH YOUR KNIFE THOROUGHLY BEFORE PROCEEDING.

WILD BOAR SKINNING, BUTCHERING, TANNING, SOFTSKIN, RAWHIDE, CANNING, DRYING AND SMOKING ARE AT THE BEGINNING OF THE BOOK.

WILD BOAR LIVER, KIDNEYS, TONGUE, BRAINS, HEART, MINCEMEAT AND SAUSAGE ARE AT THE BEGINNING OF THE BOOK.

CURING THE WILD PIG, WILD BOAR, COLLARD PECCARY, JAVELINA OR MUSK HOG

Many people feel the wild pig must be "cured". To do this, mix in a large crock:

2 cups vinegar or 1 bottle of wine
1/2 to 1 cup chopped onion
2 cloves garlic, peeled and crushed with a fork and a pinch of salt
3 bay leaves
2 teaspoons Italian seasoning, or your favorite herbs
Salt and pepper to taste

Add the meat, cover, and let stand in a cool place 38 to 40 degrees F. for one to two weeks. Each day, stir liquid and make sure all pieces of meat are covered by the marinade. Remove the meat and discard the marinade. Rinse in cool water and freeze in individual packets or proceed as follows. You may use the meat for any pork recipe you fancy.

POT ROAST OF JAVELINA OR WILD PIG

Prepare pig as instructed above, including the

Big Game

curing. In a large, heavy crock, put 3 tablespoons oil. Add 1 sliced carrot, 1 cup chopped celery, 1 large sliced onion and 1 large garlic clove which has been crushed with salt, and brown lightly. Push to one side. Rub javelina roast with 2 tablespoons cinnamon and 1/2 teaspoon cloves and brown lightly on both sides. Cover with browned vegetables, add 1 cup beef bouillon and 1 cup water, cover and put in 325 degrees F. oven for 4 hours. Turn the meat occasionally, adding more liquid if needed. Remember, NO SALT. Your meat was salted in the curing process. If the meat is a little too salty to your taste, before starting the recipe, cover it with fresh water, bring to a boil, boil 5 minutes and pour off water, then proceed with the recipe.

ROAST BABY JAVELINA OR WILD PIG

Clean the animal as instructed at the beginning of chapter one, but don't cut it up. Make any good chicken or turkey dressing, using at least 2 cups diced bread. Wash the pig carefully inside and out. Rub the inside with salt and pepper and rub with garlic cloves. Put in stuffing and close the cavity. Sew or skewer it shut. Prop the mouth open with a 2 inch block of wood. Rub the outside with cooking oil, garlic cloves and salt and pepper. Put it in a roasting pan, cavity side down. Pour 2 cups chicken broth or bouillon in the pan and COVER. Roast it $450°$ F. for 20 minutes, reduce heat to $325°$ F. and continue to roast, allowing 30 minutes for each pound, basting every 15 minutes. I find a meat thermometer indispensible for this. The internal temperature must be $175°$ F. Place a cranberry in each eye, an apple in his mouth, and garnish with parsley or watercress.

SAUTEED FILLET OF WILD PIG

Clean, skin and marinate pig as instructed above. Cut thin slices from the leg or roasts. Sprinkle with pepper and pound with a rolling pin or the back of a heavy knife until thin. Saute them over a moderately hot flame in butter or margarine and oil. (Half and half.) Serve with potato pancakes.

Game Sauces

DEVIL BARBECUE SAUCE

1/2 cup sliced or chopped onion
1/2 cup catsup
2 cloves garlic crushed by a fork with 1/4 tsp. salt
2 tablespoons Worcestershire sauce
1 teaspoon prepared mustard
1/4 cup oil
1/2 teaspoon chili powder (more or less, depending on how devilish you want to get)

SOUR CREAM SAUCE

1/2 cup sour cream
1/4 teaspoon onion salt or salt
1 tablespoon bottled onion or garlic juice

Beat together and serve cold or beat together and stir into defatted pan juices of any wild game or fowl. If you like sour cream, you'll love this simple, delicious sauce.

CHEESE SAUCE

1 can cheddar cheese soup
1/2 cup cream or undiluted evaporated milk
1/4 pound cheese, diced in small pieces
2 tablespoons sherry, if wine flavoring is wanted

Big Game

Salt and pepper to taste

Beat together cream and soup, add diced cheese and heat over low heat until cheese is half melted. (I like some cheese lumps to remain.) Taste for seasoning and pour over loaf.

HORSERADISH SAUCE

1/2 cup sour cream
1 teaspoon prepared horseradish
1 teaspoon onion juice
Onion salt to taste (Plain salt if you have no onion salt)

Beat ingredients together and serve with game.

ORANGE SAUCE

Combine:

Juices from the roasting pan
1 clove garlic, crushed
1 can undiluted chicken broth
1 can orange marmalade
2 tablespoons orange liqueur
1 tablespoon cornstarch mixed to a smooth paste with 1/4 cup water

Bring to a boil. Simmer gently for 3 minutes. Excellent with fowl.

TOMATO AND ONION SAUCE

1 can undiluted tomato soup
1 tablespoon onion juice
1/2 cup cream or undiluted evaporated milk
1 teaspoon parsley
1/2 teaspoon salt (celery or onion salt if preferred)

Heat, beat together and pour mixture over loaf.

BOILED DRESSING

Fry 2 strips of bacon and put bacon on paper towel to drain. Blend until smooth:

1 beaten egg
1/2 cup sugar
1 1/2 tablespoons flour
1 teaspoon ground mustard
1 teaspoon salt
1/4 cup vinegar
2 cups hot water or milk

Pour mixture into bacon fat and bring to a boil. turn down heat and beat with egg beater while boiling gently for 1 minute. Taste and correct seasoning. Crumble bacon in dressing.

Big Game Recipes Just For Fun

Chapter 6

I believe I have covered all I set out to cover in the correct cleaning, cooking and preserving of Big Game, therefore I will allow myself a little leeway; a little fun with recipes we may not use every day, but nevertheless enjoy.

HAGGIS

My grandfather's name was John Dewar, so I include with pride a most traditional Scottish dish.

This earned its fearsome reputation because it was originally made in the stomach bag of a sheep- washed, boiled, scraped, soaked, washed and boiled again, but a stomach bag, nonetheless. At that, it was not so different from our American sausage which was originally stuffed in the intestines of the pig. (Until the invention of modern sausage casings.)

Today, I give you Haggis in the All-American sheep's stomach substitute- the plastic brown and roast bag. (Self basting oven cooking bag)

- 1 Brown and roast bag
- ¼ lb. bacon
- 10 tablespoonfuls oatmeal
- 2 cups finely chopped, cooked or uncooked game. The liver and the "lights" were traditional.
- ¼ cup beef bouillon or gravy
- 1 finely chopped onion
- Salt and pepper to taste

Fry out bacon. Remove bacon to a paper towel and for 1 minute gently fry the chopped onion in the bacon drippings. Add the beef bouillon, oatmeal and chopped game to the pan and crumble the bacon into it. Stir well and taste for seasoning- add salt and pepper if desired. Put the mixture into the bag, making sure the bag is not over half full, as the mixure swells. Secure the bag and prick it three times with a pin, so the air can escape. Put the bag in a large pan of boiling water and simmer it gently for 1½ to 2 hours. My 100 year old recipe says "serve on a dish, without garnish or gravy, it being sufficiently rich in itself".

MARKLE CHAFING DISH VENISON

This wonderful recipe was given to me by my brother-in-law, George Markle, who said it is great fun because it can be cooked at the table in either a chafing dish or (blush, blush, lack of class but so easy) the electric fry pan.

I have found the recipe invaluable because it is so easy to use in cooking demonstrations and I have never found anyone who didn't say it tastes good, and when you're dealing with the general public, that's something.

- 1 pound game, cleaned and aged as directed, then cut into 2 inch long, 1 inch wide strips.

Big Game

¼ pound butter
½ cup wine of your choice (Port was traditional, but I prefer cream sherry.)

Incidentally, all may be served from the same bottle of wine while the dish is being prepared. Sort of prepares the palate, as it were.

¼ cup currant jelly
Salt and pepper to taste

Melt ½ of the butter in the chafing dish, or the fry--pan turned to one above simmer. Lay the strips of game in a single layer in the sizzling butter and cook for about two minutes. Add the rest of the butter and turn the meat over and cook for two or three minutes more. Gently salt and pepper the meat to taste, then add the currant jelly and the wine to the pan and stir until the jelly is melted. Let the meat simmer in the sauce for three to five minutes at the lowest possible heat setting. Correct seasoning. (This is time for a board of directors meeting among the diners. Add salt, pepper, more wine or currant jelly to everyone's taste.) Serve the dish with a large spoon so that everyone can get the wonderful butter, wine and currant jelly sauce. Brown or wild rice (depending on your pocketbook that day) is an ideal accompaniment.

If you are a teetotaler you may substitute chicken or beef bouillon for the wine.

TOAD IN THE HOLE

I told you we were going to wing it. Here goes. This is a very old Scottish dish.

1 pound properly cleaned and aged big game steak, 1 inch thick, cut into eight pieces.

Sprinkle the steak with ½ teaspoon salt and ¼ teaspoon of pepper and put it into a greased cake dish, some pieces standing on edge.

Chapter Six

Batter
2 medium sized eggs
2 cups of milk
4 tablespoons flour
1/8 teaspoon salt

Beat this all together in a blender or with beater and pour it over steak, making sure that the two or three centre pieces have their "heads" above the batter. Bake for ½ to ¾ hour in 400 degree oven, until the batter is "set" and the top is starting to brown.

BUBBLE AND SQUEAK

This is also a very old recipe and a great way to use cold roasted or boiled game.

1 pound previously cooked game, cut in slices
1/8 pound butter
3 or 4 cups cabbage, cut into medium sized pieces
1 tablespoon vinegar
Salt and pepper to taste

Melt the butter in a large frying pan. Add the meat and fry for two minutes, until just heated through. Add the chopped cabbage, sprinkle 1 teaspoon salt and ¼ teaspoon pepper over it and COVER. Turn the pan down to your lowest heat setting and fry gently for 10 minutes, until the cabbage is tender. Sprinkle the vinegar over the top, stir and serve.

POTTED GAME

I must include this recipe as it is delicious served hot or cold and is also a very old way to preserve game. It is really a paté, preserved by having melted butter poured over it.

The proportions given below may be varied. Re-

Big Game

member, always, to taste for seasoning before you press it into the mold.

1 pound cooked game
½ pound cooked ham, or, if you don't have that, ½ pound bacon, boiled for 15 minutes in barely simmering ½ cup water
1 teaspoon sugar
½ teaspoon salt, more if needed
¼ teaspoon pepper
1/8 teaspoon allspice
1/8 teaspoon mace
1 medium sized onion

If you don't have all those seasonings, don't skip this recipe. Use your own favorites.

Remove the bone, fat and gristle from the game and put it into the food processor. Add the boiled bacon, onion and seasonings and process until finely chopped. (About 20 seconds). If you do not have a food processor, you must chop eveything together, very finely. Fry a tiny amount to taste for seasoning, and adjust seasoning. Press into buttered mold or buttered glass loaf pan.

Set the dish into a bigger pan containing hot water and bake at 350 degrees for 45 minutes to 1 hour. Clarify ½ cup (1 stick) of butter by melting it in a pan, then pouring off all but the milky residue in the bottom. Pour this over the top, making sure it is covered and sealed. Keep this in the refrigerator.

You may serve it, sliced, on a lettuce leaf with buttered toast for a main luncheon dish. You may serve it, sliced and heated in butter as the meat for the main course. You may serve it sliced, hot or cold, in sandwiches. You may serve the whole loaf, hot or cold, for a buffet. A most versatile dish.

Chapter Six

I think it is very interesing to read how they treated game years ago, so here is a recipe from 1861.

ROAST HAUNCH OF VENISON 1861

INGREDIENTS- Venison, coarse flour-and-water paste, a little flour.

MODE- Choose a haunch with clear, bright, and thick fat, and the cleft of the hoof smooth and close; the greater quantity of fat there is, the better quality will the meat be. As many people object to venison when it has too much "haut gout", ascertain how long it has been kept by running a sharp skewer into the meat close to the bone: when this is withdrawn its sweetness can be judged of. With care and attention, it will keep good a fortnight, unless the weather is very mild. Keep it perfectly dry by wiping it with clean cloths till not the least damp remains, and sprinkle over powdered ginger or pepper, as a preventative against the fly. When required for use, wash it in warm water, and dry it well with a cloth; butter a sheet of white paper, put it over the fat, lay a coarse paste, about 1/2 inch in thickness, over this, and then a sheet or two of strong paper. Tie the whole firmly on to the haunch with twine, and put the joint down to a strong close fire; baste the venison immediately, to prevent the paper and string from burning, and continue this operation, without intermission, the whole of the time it is cooking. About 20 minutes before it is done, carefully remove the paste and paper, dredge the joint with flour, and baste well with butter until it is nicely frothed, and of a nice pale-brown colour; garnish the knuckle--bone with a frill of white paper, and serve with a good, strong, but unflavoured gravy, in a tureen, and currant jelly; or melt the jelly with a little port wine, and serve that also in a tureen. As the principal object in roasting venison is to preserve the fat, the above is

Big Game

the best mode of doing so where expense is not objected to; but, in ordinary cases, the paste may be dispensed with and a double paper placed over the roast instead; it will not require so long cooking without the paste. Do not omit to send very hot plates to table, as the venison fat so soon freezes: to be thoroughly enjoyed by epicures, it should be eaten on hot-water plates. The neck and shoulder may be roasted in the same manner.

TIME- A large haunch of buck-venison, with the paste, 4 to 5 hours; haunch of doe-venison, 3 1/4 to 3 3/4 hours. Allow less time without the paste.

AVERAGE COST 1s,6d. to 1s. 8d. per lb
Sufficient for 18 persons.

A Brief History of Using Fire to Prepare Meat (and a very early recipe)

A brief history of preparing meat, using fire, was given by Isabella Beeton in her "The Book of Household Management", published in 1861.

The neolithic, or second stone age possesses marked peculiarities of its own; polished stone implements made their appearance, domestic animals were used, and cooking their flesh began.

Fire having been discovered, mankind endeavoured to make use of it for drying, and afterwards for cooking their meat; but they were a considerable time before they hit upon proper and commodious methods of employing it in the preparation of their food.

Meat, then, placed on burning fuel was found better than when raw; it had more firmness, was eaten with less difficulty, and the ozmazome being condensed by the carbonization, gave it a pleasing perfume and flavour. Still, however, the meat cooked on the coal would become somewhat befouled, certain portions of the fuel adhering to it. This disadvantage was remedied by passing spits through it, and placing it at a suitable height above the burning fuel.

In Homer's time the art of cookery had not ad-

Big Game

vanced much beyond this; for we read in the "Iliad", how the great Achilles and his friend Patroclus regaled the three Grecian leaders on bread, wine, and broiled meat. It is noticeable, too, that Homer does not speak of boiled meat anywhere in his poems. Later, however, the Jews coming out of their captivity in Egypt, had made much greater progress. They undoubtedly possessed kettles; and in one of these, Esau's mess of pottage, for which he sold his birthright, must have been prepared.

Brillat Savarin tells the story of a Croat captain, whom he invited to dinner in 1815, during the occupation of Paris by the allied troops. This officer was amazed at his host's preparations, and said, "When we are campaigning, and get hungry, we knock over the first animal we find, cut off a steak, powder it with salt, which we always have in the sabretasche, put it under the saddle, gallop over it for half a mile, and then dine like princes."

Now that is MACHO!

In Defense of Hunting (Or, Ann Landers Eat Your Heart Out)

From Isabella Beeton's "The Book of Household Management" published in 1861, comes a most astute observation.

"Far, far away in ages past, our fathers loved the chase, and what it brought; and it is usually imagined that when Isaac ordered his son Esau to go out with his weapon, his quiver and his bow, and to prepare for him savoury meat, such as he loved, that it was venison he desired. The wise Solomon, too, delighted in this kind of fare; for we learn that, at his table, every day were served the wild ox, the roebuck, and the stag. Xenophon informs us, in his History, that Cyrus, King of Persia ordered that venison should never be wanting at his repasts; and of the effeminate Greeks it was the delight. The Romans, also, were devoted admirers of the flesh of the deer; and our own kings and princes, from the Great Alfred down to the late Prince Consort, have hunted, although, it must be confessed, under vastly different circumstances, the swift buck, and relished their "haunch" all the more keenly, that they had borne themselves bravely in the pursuit of the animal."

Continuing, "From (their) days down to the present, the sports of the field have continued to hold their

Big Game

high reputation, not only for the promotion of health, but for helping to form that manliness of character which enters so largely into the composition of the sons of the British soil. That it largely helps to do this there can be no doubt. The late Duke of Grafton, when hunting, was, on one occasion, thrown into a ditch. A young curate, engaged in the same chase, cried out, "Lie still, my lord!" leapt over him, and pursued his sport. Such an apparent want of feeling might be expected to have been resented by the duke; but not so. On his being helped up by his attendant, he said, "That man shall have the first good living that falls to my disposal: had he stopped to have given me his sympathy, I never would have given him anything." Such was the manly sentiment of the duke, who delighted in the exemplification of a spirit similarly ardent as his own in the sport, and above the baseness of an assumed sorrow."

And to repeat myself, from Genesis 9: 2 & 3, "And the fear of you and the dread of you shall be upon every beast of the earth, and upon every fowl of the air, upon all that moveth upon the earth, and upon all the fishes of the sea; into your hand are they delivered. Every moving thing that liveth shall be meat for you; even as the green herb have I given you all things."

Everything that lives must have the will to live. I believe that the smallest blade of grass desires to grow, flourish, reproduce and enjoy good health under ideal circumstances: but none is successful in this determination indefinitely. Every Body, plant or animal, is taken by death to be used in the sustenance of other bodies. If Truth is Absolute Reality, this statement is a truth of the basic condition of our visible universe.

If we abhor and fear Death, we abhor and fear our world, our universe.

Either the intelligent energy who created this world has committed a grave error, or our perception of this world is a grave error. I leave that for you to figure out.

Index

Aging	11
Antelope - general	49, 50
Cleaning	49, 50
Roast	50
Shish kabob	51
Steaks	50
Arizona Desert bighorn sheep - see Sheep	60, 61
Bear- General	61-64
Fat rendering	63
Marinade	62
Roast loin of bear	63
Steak	64
Stew	64
Bighorn - see Sheep	60, 61
Bison - see Buffalo	55-57
Boiled Dressing	69
Brains	42
Braised Pot Roast	56
Bubble and Squeak	73
Buckskin - making	33-35
Buffalo	55-57
Barbecue	57
Steaks	56, 57
Butchering	12-20
Buttered Rice with Herbs	52

Index

Canning	21-23
Cheese Sauce	67
Collard Peccary - see Pig	64-67
Corned	42
Corned, Simple	43
Dall Sheep - see Sheep	60, 61
Deer	53-55
Drying	23-25
Meat Loaf	53, 54
Pan Broiled Steaks	54
Stroganoff Chops	55
Defense of Hunting	79-81
Devil Barbecue Sauce	67
Drying	23, 24, 25
Elk	51-53
Foil Roasted	53
Sweet & Sour Ribs	52
Swiss Steak	52
Fried Bread	55
Goat	57, 58
Kebabs	58
Roast	58
Gunracks	36
Gutting - Big Game	1-6
Haggis	70
Hard Hide Curing	36
Heart-Cleaning	41
Sauteed	42
Stuffed	41
History of Cooking Wild Game	77-78
Horseradish Sauce	68
Javelina - see Pig	64-67
Jerky	23, 24
Kidneys	37
Broiled	37

Index

Cleaning	37
Pan Fried	38
Liver - Braised	40
Braised & Sour Cream	41
Cleaning	39
Spread	40
With Bacon	40
Marinade	49
Markle Chafing Dish Venison	71, 72
Mincemeat	44
Moose	58, 59
Roast with Chestnuts	59
Sausage	59
Mountain Goat - see Goat	57, 58
Musk Hog - See Pig	64-67
Orange Sauce	68
Potted Game	73, 74
Pig	64-67
Curing	65
Pot Roast	65, 66
Roast	66
Sauteed Fillet	66-67
Pronghorn - See Antelope	49-51
Rawhide	35
Rawhide Laces	35
Rawhide Window Glass	35-36
Rice - Buttered with Herbs	52
Roast Haunch of Venison, 1861	75, 76
Rocky Mountain Goat - see Goat	57, 58
Rocky Mountain Sheep - see Sheep	60, 61
Salting - Brine	25
Salting - Dry	26
Sauces	67-69
Boiled Dressing	69
Cheese Sauce	67

Index

Devil Barbecue Sauce	67
Horseradish Sauce	68
Orange Sauce	68
Sour Cream Sauce	67
Tomato & Onion Sauce	68
Sausage	46-47
Sheep	60, 61
Roast	60
Roast (Young)	60, 61
Skinning - Conventional	6-8
Skinning - Trophy Mount	8-10
Smokehouse	27-31
Smoking - General	27-32
Sour Cream Sauce	67
Spareribs	45
Charcoal Barbecue	46
Oven Barbecue	46
Stuffed	45
Stone Sheep - see Sheep	60, 61
Tanning	32-35
Toad in a Hole	72
Tomato & Onion Sauce	68
Tongue - Cleaning	38
Boiled	38
Braised	39
Breaded	39
Venison - General Directions	48
Wild Boar - see Pig	64-67
Window Glass (Rawhide)	35

Epilogue

Somehow, society must be more realistically rearranged to allow us to use our God given right to sustain ourselves. Hungry people who live in the city can be arrested for killing and eating pigeons, while the birds proliferate until they are a threat to public health. Madness!

Thousands of teen-age children, as well as younger children, could add to their families' well-being by hunting and fishing, but they are denied the opportunity by unrealistic hunting and fishing laws. Even in big cities, fishing could be done in the rivers and the ocean and many birds and some other wild life is available. To demand a hunting or fishing license for anyone under the age of 18 is immoral. How better could young people be occupied?

Also, a welfare card or a senior citizen's card should be a legal hunting and fishing license.

If we have a reverence for life we must have a reverence for death. God created both; but in death he provided for an infinite number of ways for death to sustain life. It may be what the universe is all about.

What a Gift!

If you know anyone who hunts or fishes, they'd probably love a copy of these books. Share with them the mouth-watering recipes and simple cleaning instructions for all types of game, fish and fowl. It makes an inexpensive and thoughtful gift.

Simply fill in the coupon below and enclose a check or money order for $9.95 (+ $1.00 postage and handling). We'll send a copy to you in a matter of weeks.

Please send me The Complete Encyclopedia of Wild Game & Fish Cleaning & Cooking. I'm enclosing $9.95 for each 3 volume set I order, plus $1.00 postage and handling.
PA residents add 6% sales tax.

Amount Enclosed .... # of Book Sets ....
Send to: Yesnaby Publishers, RD 8, Box 213, Danville PA 17821

Name _____
Address _____
City _____
State _____Zip _____